SALT MARSH DIARY

A Year on the Connecticut Coast

MARK SETH LENDER

ST. MARTIN'S PRESS
New York

www.stmartins.com

Book design and illustration by Kathryn Parise

LIBRARY OF CONGRESS CATALOGING-IN-PUBLICATION DATA

Lender, Mark Seth.
    Salt marsh diary : a year on the Connecticut coast / Mark Seth Lender.—1st ed.
            p. cm.
    ISBN 978-0-312-65601-0
    1. Salt marsh ecology—Connecticut—Anecdotes.   2. Salt marsh animals—Connecticut—Anecdotes.   3. Salt marshes—Connecticut—Anecdotes.   I. Title.
    QH105.C8L46 2011
    598.1776909746—dc22
                                                    2010035796

First Edition: April 2011

10 9 8 7 6 5 4 3 2 1

For Valerie,

all these words, and all the words

that are to come. . . .

Who can wait quietly while the mud settles?

—Lao Tzu, *Tao Te Ching*
(translated by Gia-Fu Feng)

ACKNOWLEDGMENTS

Without the persistent dedication and commitment of Peter Riva, this book would never have seen the light of day. I also want to thank Eileen Bolinsky for finding value in my voice and for providing me a place from which to be heard.

Above all, I owe a profound debt of gratitude to Alice Quinn, who had faith in me and in this work long before I did.

Prologue

This is where I live: Salt marsh bounded by rivers East and West that empty and fill with the tide. Sometimes the marsh is flooded, spartina and sedges buried in a lake of brackish water. Sometimes, as in winter, that grass looks desert dry, sun bleached and yellow and only late in spring will it green again. South, the marsh is protected by dunes from the sea, an animal who roars in storms and rocks as a cradle rocks in calm weather. Opposite, the wetland narrows to a finger pointing north. As the rivers dissipate toward their source, marsh gives way to the remnant of granite mountains, once great, now worn down. The woods there are mostly silent. It is here on low forgotten ground, grudgingly protected from dredge and fill, from Profit, from loss, it is here that life abounds. This is where I stand.

SPRING

Seeds with Wings

The salt marsh on these drab Spring mornings has the cast and texture of a close-cropped head. Thick. Brushed. Tan wetted to brown and the river parts it like a razor. But the marsh is done with its winter cut and beneath, seed takes root. It is a thing you cannot prove. It is something which you know. You know it by sound. By the odor of the air. By light and the adjective of sky which today is different. You can feel it. Even the skin has eyes.

Now down the river an osprey comes on a volute of air, spiraling. All his attention is focused below. He hovers ready to plant himself to water but finds no fertile place, nothing to make him grow. He sees me, a brief flash, recognition of a kind words cannot define, and goes. And with his departure the light changes also to a filtered gold. It is a tentative light and will not last. It does not matter. The feeling that has drawn me is still there and though it is fine to see the osprey he is not what I came for. I know this. I know it is elsewhere. Where I cannot say because I am not sure, of what it is, that I am seeking. But then I am sure: I am looking for Cedar Waxwings.

It is hard to explain where they come from, these knowledges. They sprout. Unfolding leaves and petals that are understood though not identified until fully opened and revealed. One thing they never are is a contentment.

The remains of the day is a fruitless searching. A pair of mallards let me come impossibly close and only then announce their irritation, blasting away in a snap of feathers. Crossing the salt meadow to the beach, I see a flock of canvasbacks bobbing a half mile out, their reddish heads black in the distance where they glide in the swell above the middle shallows. The local mergansers, six of a possible seven, dally between the spiles warily while I pass. I had not noticed them, distracted by that small and effable thing planted among the senses as if waiting for water, waiting for sun, sotto voce: Cedar Waxwings.

The light is all but gone. Unfulfilled, this at once geotropic, heliotropic urge shrivels and is discarded. It is all absence now. Sore from hours of walking and of standing still I amble down the rough, water-gouged ravine that is our driveway to the usual din of small birds in the evergreens, sparrows no doubt, not really worth remarking and I don't. Except—*that something*—some flash some tone some color at the corner of perception makes me raise my eyes to find—Cedar Waxwings!

They flitter among the juniper, burying in the branches, eating the dusted bluepurple berries, touching close, unconcerned, talking to themselves as they dine. I cannot tell which is their leader. He would be the one who in flight, constantly chattering, moves around the edges of the flock keeping them in line, telling them how and why. Then without apparent cue they fly up (he must have given them a sign) and settle in the spruce across the way, and they primp and adjust themselves leisurely it seems until some second signal comes, and they are gone.

❦

I cannot remember entering the house. Or wandering to the window. I do remember staring out and how I felt when against an overcast sky twelve returning great blue herons flew by, over water, way out. Where they are going, what seed they will sow when at long last they land even they cannot tell.

❦

Wings and Earth

A bird is a seed with wings
but the earth does not love her
she sprouts only by spreading her leaves
in skies plowed by the wind

—EUGEN JEBELEANU

From the collection Secret Weapon, *translated from the Romanian by Matthew Zapruder and Radu Ioanid and used by permission.*

Form Follows Function

The beach is littered with glacial irregulars, the going is slow. Between these huge gray stones not a footprint in the pebbly sand. No evidence of human hand except, just inshore, the rusted rebar and waste concrete, all that remains of an outpost left from the Just War. It survived the German submarines but not the weather. The stunted trees, the tangle of *Rosa rugosa*, the sedge and sedum rooted among the blue and silver shoals of mussel shells, these endure, not so much because they hold fast but that they lay low. Only the birds call this place Home.

On a bare sumac Black-crowned Night Herons land. The snipped and snapped branches, demolished in the storms of winter and summer hold them lightly. They've nested below (an island still in isolation, there are no predators here) and the treetops, such as they are, afford more risk from wind than safety. So the herons climb only for the vantage, clear to all sides, where they can see, me, and do not like it.

There are seven in all, a small flock magnified by these close quarters. They want me to know the place is theirs and glare, expecting me to turn away. I don't, and their frustration grows until they take it out on each other (in the way spouse yells at mate who punishes child who torments the family dog). Except, of separate families, the herons are more of a clutch or a clan. It is my blood they'd like to draw and because they can't, internecine conflict is the result. Beaks seek feathers as they pick and peck and flare their wings and one by one, drive their neighbors out.

We are down to a moody Nairobi Trio. They sulk in silence exchanging dirty looks. Just as well. What they'd say to me is no doubt unprintable. I would take the hint too except I want what I came for, squinting down the barrel of the biggest hunk of glass I can carry waiting for that perfect shot which will be—when the bird at the very top of the tree, clear of the clutter, takes wing. Twenty minutes; twenty-five; The lens grows heavy as a lead pipe. My hands shake. The sun is on broil. The mosquitoes are calling their friends and relations to the free lunch that is the back of my neck.

Finally, the only one left is that one bird and me. We stand our ground in mutual irritation like gunslingers in a Spaghetti Western (the heron is Clint Eastwood. I'm the guy who grimaces and sweats). And then, smack-in-the-middle-of-the-forehead, I get it: The *top bird* is the Top Bird.

Black-crowned night herons, aside from being territorial are hierarchical. Positions are earned not inherited and must be maintained. Dominant birds know this, and each act of aggression toward a subaltern is a reinforcement, a literal *keeping down*. The roosting tree is its graphical representation. Stressed, the articulations are revealed as ranks depart, in inverse order, bottommost first.

Having proved his point the last heron lets go. The shutter clicks. The heron calls that clipped chuckle of a call— one, last, laugh.

On Mother's Day

A Red-bellied Woodpecker purrs her trill just above my head. There is no need to look. I know her. Then, out pops that completely alizarin crimson head from a small round hole and Her is a He.

The nest is up in a dead birch, too near the top to look inside. You don't have to. You know there are eggs there, small, bright as an eye, waiting. He guards them with his life. This also is a father's work in Spring.

But if there are no limits to self-sacrifice, hunger is its own device. Without food, even he cannot do what he must and he knows it. So he calls, entreating to his mate to come and relieve him until finally he hears that loud, teakettle banging high in the canopy that is the steamy song of woodpecker love. But this drummer girl belongs to someone else, and though he trills and trills and purrs his pleadings again and again his own does not return to him. Eventually need weakens will. The rest of him emerges, and clinging to the bark moves all around its narrow girth, searching for insects there. He has done this many times before and there is little to find. He would do better further away but Fatherhood is his tether. He calls the more.

Besides food there are other reasons for being outside today. There is light, and warmth of the sun after a long night, and above all the need to stretch the better part of which is a good scratch. "Good" in woodpecker parlance is *thorough*. There is hardly a corner missed. A wing salutes to be preened and cleaned. Feet meet chin. Beak (fortuitously long) meets breast, neck flexible as a rubber band brings beak to back. A simple dust bath would be easier and more efficient or better still a quick dash and a splash at the edge of the pond below, but the tether does not extend nearly so far, and he cannot go.

Some say once the eggshell cracks the strong brace of mate and mate, of parent and parented will wane, then weaken, then irrevocably cease. I find that hard to believe. So much dire attention paid, how could any one forget the other? From Red-bellied Woodpecker to Red-bellied Woodpecker, what loyalties tap, sound as a signal drum in empty winter woods? Such a bond must be more enduring than a change in the weather. Cannot be forgot in the cold and winter dark, that brief awaiting of Spring's spark. Indeed a nest of the previous year stands above the one they've nested now confirming, they've loved here before, and will the more.

There is one other possibility. Spring has been late. Birds have arrived later still, birds of every kind. Perhaps the nest he guards so assiduously is empty. Perhaps all his entreaty is just that, the predicate of hope unrealized and nothing more. No one has come to join him. He sits alone and lonely dreams of love and progeny which have not come. May never come.

Again he calls, and waits, and none appears nor is there any answer.

The Loon

Loon sails silent across the little waves, more through than over them. Large-headed, hooded in black, a thick neck made for swallowing not the bait plucked by the stabbing of herons, not the tiny crabs and bottom creatures captured by the mergansers, but great fishes—whales of fishes—fishes that thrash and fume and smack the water into foam. As sure as a doryman's gill net cast in shallow water Loon repairs, just there, off the near bar where he dives effortless as a stone, ripples spreading so slow they disappear long before they reach the shore. And he holds his breath so long. And he swims so far. And down and down he goes, to bob up, blinking. Then does not gasp, or rest, as if he has made no effort except, having broken the common hunger of the mouth he seines the sea far-reaching with his eyes against the solitary hunger of the soul.

Seeking for another of his kind, he does not find.

Much of the year I see Loon, always by himself. Near shore, in and out about the rough-tumbled boulders of the terminal moraine he goes, alert, at home, as if his ancient arctic self responds to these artifacts of ice long gone. When the great river beneath the glacier roared, when the bergs cleaved like the fractured limbs of giants he was there, to hear, to see, to record and remember in the hollows of his bones. Even now when the lap and lick of the ocean is musical, soft as a whisper, cold is all he knows.

I cannot imagine Loon in Summer. Even his presence in Spring seems incongruent here upon this vast Atlantic as unforgiving as the edge of the world. Among rolling seas where Loon makes his ascent and traverse it always must be Winter. I sometimes think this is what Loon also believes. In his silence. In his self-counsel. In the fastness of his frigid sleep.

Always alone.

That was when Loon surprised me, after I thought I knew him completely. The light was almost gone, the songs of evening subsided and Loon came alive. In syntony with fog and the glittering blackness, long, deep in the throat, a sound into solution with the dark wet air, I hear it now in my mind, as if for the first time, *A — ah — Loon! A — ah — Loon!* I cannot see him. I only hear him. Somewhere in the off-shore, a voice that rises to falsetto and the low slow glide. *A — ah — Loon! A — ah — Looon!* And this would be enough that the silence is broken but the tremolo of a soulmate follows, call and answer, answer and call, joined now by others till they are everywhere, an expected prayer that will continue till the end of all that is worth remembering. *A — ah — Loon! A — ah — Looon!*

Finally it is not Loon but only me, bagged in this intractable human skin, the echo within, Alone Alone. This, while the True Self knows that every atom of our being was forged in the core of stars, Alive, Aware, Alike to the Oneness of All Things. The night rings.

A — ah — Loooon! A — ah — Loooon!

The Few,
the Brave and Lucky Few

R ed-winged Blackbird stands sentry all day. Before
sun up till long after the sun goes down with only a
few seeds to sustain him and these seldom taken, he is
pure vigilance. "See-me," he sings, "Seeee-me," a song that
changes only when something catches his eye, something which should not be there, something too close.
"Looook..." he warns, "Look...Look...Looook..."
Then, "What? What? What-was-that?" But it's nothing,
the shadow of a passing cloud, a puff of wind against a
blade of grass, a leaf falling. Soon enough he's back to that
signature "Seeee-me!"

This little bird, would-be cynosure of all the world he knows, seems ridiculous in his bravado. Not so. From the cover of brush at the edge of the marsh comes an enormous crow, glistening and purple-black on head and back and flying slow. The crow decides on a shortcut over the near spartina. Mistake. He does not notice Redwing returning from a recent false alarm to his perch at the top of the near dead cedar. Now midflight, Redwing reverses course. The blazes on his wings flashing fire he is on that crow like thunder.

"GET! GET! GET!"

Redwing cries his cri de guerre and loops and dives and dives again, clipping black feathers with quick sharp blows of tiny-taloned feet. The Battle of Britain might have looked like this, Spitfires pealing off to meet the lumbering Junkers 88s, maneuverability and nerve matched against muscle and death. For the crow is destroyer to the nest and as sure as any mercenary among the invading horde, he will plunder if he can. More than once I've seen him with a baby bird limp in his beak. It is his way, he cannot help it. So his reputation is deserved, so Redwing's vigil is well-founded.

The crow for all his strength and wit is clumsy in defense and must give way. He raises wings at an awkward angle attempting to fend off, only to be tagged again and again until sliding away that crow is finally, gratefully out of range.

Redwing returns to his place. Below, at least three

nests still safe, for his guardianship extends to other families beside his own. "Look at ME!" he sings, in the same triumphal tones, "come look at ME!" And if the egret dares to share a branch on Redwing's tree he will be challenged, and the little green heron if he lands too close. Nor is the osprey, nearly a fathom wing-to-wing, any match for this corsair and the blood-red decal that he wears. It is not pride upon his sleeve, but heart.

Redwing gives no ground. He does not fear. He will not yield.

Killdeer, Mistress of Deceptions

Killdeer keeps a catalogue of deceptions. A triangle of feathers at the back of her head plumbs nub to nape, sharply to a point. At a glance (or even more than a glance) you'd probably mistake it for a beak. An illusion made all the more complete by white bushy brows over large amber eyes that round beyond her cheeks as if, she looks in all directions at once. You never know if she is facing you or not, if she sees you or she doesn't. Quite the defense if you're a predator, one among the many toothy things come by stealth to attack, like a tiger attacks, from behind. And which way is that ... Can't tell? Good. For such is the weird she intended. Bobcat sneaking up on her does not know which way to sneak. Owl cannot be sure if she is coming, or going. Fox is outfoxed.

Killdeer is just as confusing forward as in reverse. Whimsy is the mask she wears, broad zebra stripes, brown and white on her head and breast to obscure and unhinge her features. How far, how big, which way, all are momentary matters of conjecture and in that moment's hesitation she makes her magical escape.

Trusting to wit and kit Killdeer nests on open ground. One, nearby, chooses the parched and grassy plain within a traffic circle for her home. I suppose the dark ribbon of the roadway seems to her more like a mote of water than hard tarmac, or perhaps a riverbed gone dry—an ideal demesne in which to raise a family, in Killdeer's economy. As to the nest itself, a shallow bowl paved with bits of shell and stone, it offers no protection. Her sole bulwark there is stillness, her hiding place the silted browns of her body against the dry redoubt of where she lies.

As I came close she fluttered away crying "Ki-deeel Ki-deeel" and from underneath her drab and static coat came a fan of oranges and whites outlined to make them bright and draw the eye, feigning a broken wing. Expecting me to follow she sacrificed herself, in lieu of something else: there in the nest four perfect eggs. Mottled markings random as splattered mud decorate a shell that would be white except for that tint, the slightest hint of faded green. It is a patina Rodin would have admired, a perfect joint with Nature.

Some weeks later that patina was put to a sad test. Three eggs were gone without a trace, not a bit of shell or even a stain and Killdeer nowhere to be found. Left by itself a single egg remained. Three successive afternoons I returned to where it lay intact and undisturbed. No predator, not even the sharp-eyed crows had found it there, abandoned and cold.

On the fourth day much to my relief I rediscovered Killdeer and her surviving chicks, three in number, perfect miniatures of their mother. On my approach they tucked under her wings, all except their tiny feet, like children below an umbrella. This was the last of her tricks but the baby birds had an angle of their own. Breaking free, they split in diametrically opposed directions. Had I been the animal they feared I never could have captured more than one.

The camouflage of Killdeer comes in threes, The Nape, the Stripes, the Broken Wing and then three more, the Stillness she achieves upon the nest, the Disappearing Egg which hides itself even when unguarded, the Symmetry when babies flee. Over and above is her heart, which if not unbreakable, is undefeated.

The Mother of All Mothers

Mallards begin to pair when Fall is still new. By the end of November the bachelor flights of the drakes, green heads aglow in the shallow light, are already rare. Ducks in two by two become the rule. This is how they winter through. Come April, they nest in the tufts of wild grasses beyond the brackish eddies. While the hen lays, the drake loafs at a distance not out of laziness but to draw unwelcome eyes and keep the malign at bay. It does not last. While the work of protecting the nest is a shared one, it ends in these early days. Soon after the eggs are laid the drake drifts away.

It is the hen who rules the nest and it is on her the

hatchling young will depend with an attachment of life and death. She will be to them the Mother of All Ducks. Never was there anyone more loyal, selfless and true than she of drab feathers. There is nothing she will not do for them.

Brooding by herself and far from where she feeds, it is not till May that the quiet and her loneliness break to the crack and pip of hatching. Hours later, flightless and barely dry the new ducklings sport the start of what will be their true colors only in the brown that daubs their yellow baby down. But they enter the world open-eyed and they can swim, and a good thing too, because the Mother of All Ducks is on the move.

Looking for the new, the Mother of All Ducks faces all the fear and danger of any expatriation to a foreign shore. Anxiety tenses every muscle and every muscle strains, for her family is literally in tow. Not five not ten but twelve ducklings come pedaling in a line. They cleave to one side of the V of her wake tugged along behind her, the drag nearly pulls her under. Even so, how fast she goes! She will not stop until they are landed, safely to their new home. Unbound from the place where they were born they will be borne by water where she will care for them until they fly away.

Would that we all had such mothers. Wouldn't the world be a better place?

Origin of Species

Hunter stalking the banks, eating like there's no to-morrow: Where does it all go? Any crab who lifts his head, Fiddler or Atlantic Blue will regret it. Nor is the Hermit safe in his hermitage. Yellow-crowned Night Heron consumes them all with an appetite that is bottomless, and for a reason.

Nearby a grand oak grows, the lowest limb thirty feet off the ground. Its canopy is well founded. The root secure. Windowed in a frame of green leaves the babies' heads pop up, long-necked (like half-scale giraffes or ostriches except they have no eyelashes), a look not much different from all young herons. Only the thickness of that bill is their tell. Built for crunching and cracking more than seining or stabbing they can only be Yellow-crowns. The hunting heron is their mother. Soon she will be here.

Less than a quarter mile from river, salt marsh and the shore the nest tree is in a perfect place. Yellow-crowns like shade and there is plenty of that, and the height and the density of foliage also make for safety. The fact that all this is in someone's backyard is the part that is hard to ignore but the herons have ignored it, returned now for their third round of breeding. And, where there was one nest now there are two. Between them six babies, two clutches of three, well and alive.

To keep two broods is full-time work for four parents. Crabs carried in the crop are already broken up and partly digested. Rather than mouth-to-mouth, they offload this cargo like dump trucks plunk in the center of the nest. The refuse scattered on the ground will tell you why. The large chunks of carapace, both shell and claw, mean most of the meal was utterly indigestible. You cannot force all that debris down those little throats, it must be picked and pecked and consumed by each chick as best as can. It is an effort for the adults to supply such a diet and so much of it. But the formula is successful, and the outcome will be that down turns to feathers and finally to plumage.

Safe and sound and lucky, over the months the backyard youngsters will prosper. The baby-blue egg, neatly cracked all around as if by an aesthete breakfasting from a porcelain cup, seems so small now. The baby leaping from limb to limb is so tall, as tall as he will ever be.

At last Mom arrives and despite their size the babies try to hunker low and shiver. That gesture, which is at once submission and the frisson of pleasure, is found in species as divergent from herons as kittens and sparrows. What history, what origin that so many creatures do that dance? How different from the baby elephant's caress, the baby human's smile?

Too Cute for Words

Beneath the sheltering overhang, Barn Swallows tend their young. Both parents share the work though it is more than work. It is obsession. From first light in widening circles they head out in search of food. The effort is continuous. They sweep and glide in giddy arcs made more magnificent by contrast to their tiny size, sharp blue wing and rounded umber chest flashing by. The skill, taking insects on the fly, is a combination of what can be taught and what took ten million years to learn.

Every sortie begins and ends at the nest. A dull construction made of spittle and mud it clings to the place where it was built as stuck as glue. Inside, the baby birds,

barely feathered, wait noiselessly—until a parent appears.
Then, cacophony. The chorus of their little voices is like
the grating of sand on glass.

So it's
    (1) To the brood
And
    (2) Down the hatch
And
    (3) Off again and even then that gob is never full.

When the parents leave the babes jockey for position.
This particular pair of swallows have a tendency to feed
their offspring from the same direction, right to left, moving along that always hungry line to each in turn. Which
only encourages the strongest and most audacious to
switch on subsequent feedings from first place, to second,
then third, and finally fourth for all the extras he or she
can glom. The parents are fooled only some of the time
but there is always one a little larger than the others. If
politeness counts it is not here.

Meanwhile the ones not fed righteously bellow, each
louder than their fellows. And it goes like this all day and
it does not stop till dark for even in twilight, when a min-
iscule prey is that much more invisible, still the parents
strive to feed these toothless sharks they bore, who's only
word is MORE!

Swallows if they dream must dream of gaping mouths.

Though they bear their burden in silence I think that they would comment if they could, they just don't have the time. Such is nature's trick: Parents spend the coin of their lives that progeny will survive.

The Fly

Something has died in the entryway, something small I hope because I cannot find it. With luck, a field mouse come to his end in ripe old age. Why he could not oblige by a final resting place with a better view I do not know. But here he is, locked away forever in the ceiling or the walls and aside from the smell, which is singularly unpleasant, there are already Flies.

We do not kill spiders in this house. We lead them outside or leave them alone. Only the bedroom is off limits, and even there the Daddy Longlegs has his dispensation. Hornets also find reprieve, a cup, a capture, a quick flick of the wrist at an open window sets them free. They

were here before us and will be after, allowed to stay because they belong. Flies receive no such graces. I murder
every one I can.

In contrast to that small indoor unpleasantness, the
outside is wonderful today. The dogwoods have come
out, mostly white and here and there that skin-tone blush
more peaches than cream. The cherries too are flower-
ing, red as lips, and the beach plumb, branches in dusty
bloom, from small bush all the way up to small tree. The
first of the lilacs are in bud, purple and that thin indefin-
able blue. Crocus petals of violet cupping stamens of saf-
fron, daffodils in lemon yellow and along the old stone
wall lily of the valley, a tiny unremarkable white but a
scent as strong as the most edible of colors.

All this brilliance and it owes its existence to . . . Flies.

Easy to forget Fly precedes Flower. When the first
cycads cast their spore upon the wind, blanketing the air
and the backs of scaly amphibians, even before the dino-
saurs Fly was there. Buzzing and darting between the
fronds were ugly scavengers drawn by putrefaction and
decay, and killer dragons with eight-inch wings, and mites
and midges and spiders small as pins (known to us only
in amber). All these lived in worlds of chlorophyllic green
that in its ubiquity they could not help but ignore. Then,
by fluke, some lucky plant produced among the drab a
patch of chrome, and to that wavelength novel as the
best beginning ever writ, Fly came home.

Only after eons did the Clan of Fly become the Bee,

Evolution's two-step of insect and bloom. In memory of which I open up the door, and grant reprieve to that most annoying Mother of All Forms, charmless Kali with hairy arms.

Everybody Eats

These late Spring days when first light comes so early even the bedroom windows blink and squint, all I want to do is pull the covers over my head. That's when the birds begin, drumming me to break fast. It is not an invitation to eat. It is an invitation to cook. For *them*. I'm the one who has not had his coffee and they are the ones who are grumpy. "Come and get it" is all they want to hear, finest spread North of the Border, this diner opens when the customers order.

"Whiskey dry!" I put the breadcrumbs out.

"Birdseed hold the Baby!" bowlfuls of safflower and

sunflower straight from the box, this client needs no milk
on his breakfast cereal.

First to arrive, it's always the Cardinals. They grab and
run as if they have schedules and a clock to punch. Next
the White-breasted Nuthatch. Not a regular. Used to
dine at the tree across the street but he's comin' 'round.
Spying his meal with just one eye, he'd turn his bill to the
side, awkward and slow. After a week he's learned the
common technique, a barely parted beak dainty as chop-
sticks, very neat. Next in line, Dark-eyed Junkos and a
whole gang of Tree Sparrows. Ground feeders, they are
accustomed now to the narrow counter of the porch rail,
though they scrape and scratch their feet to get at what
they want. Food everywhere!

"Hey! Ya gonna be a slob? Go take ya picnic somewhere's else."

But it's okay—the Mourning Doves jump on what
the Junkos leave behind and clean up every scrap.

"Sharp-shinned Hawk!" the Bluejay cries. Birds dive
for the bushes like the joint's been raided and whisper
when they talk, thin high whistles of warning. Some are
always caught, feathers settling on the front walk. The
Mourning Doves truly have a thing to mourn this
morning.

Rain. The place empties out. I get to sit, looking forward to a quiet second shift when, in a New York Minute,
pandemonium—Everybody starvin' all at once!

"86 that Cup a Mud ta go, Crow don't want it anyways. Bottled water? We got City Juice, take it or leave it!"

By the end of the day all I've earned is dirty dishes, and just when it's time to kill the lights, the Cardinals dash in for one last bite before I pull the mat up for the night.

But the Proprietor—that's me—knows business is business, it all adds up, I take in all the custom I can. Even that pesky Gray Squirrel rates a Blue Plate Special.

Everybody eats when they come to my house.

The Balance Bar

Mourning doves hit the windows like snowballs—
Thut-dup-dup!

—and leave the powder imprints of their passage there, chalk outline on the pane. They know about the glass even if they cannot see it but the only direction they recall just now is—*Away.*

And the thing that they are fleeing comes silent, a hush of air across his burnished wings. And they fly like the break of a summer storm, scatter like green leaves torn by wind, high to the siren whistling of their wings, and it is all the same. For the single one pursued, *far* is never far enough.

Through Spring and Summer the doves grow fat. At

the feeder they are querulous and greedy. One dove will chase the other that he or she will have none, the aggressor going without to accomplish it, and this in a world of plenty. If it were not for the eggshells lying here and there, split like bookends, you would think their only purpose was to eat. It is indeed a deadly sin. Like Cortez's Conquistadores, the gold in their pockets weighs them down.

And the last dove is racing fast and low across the spartina, wings beating like the chambers of her heart, the Cooper's hawk a heartbeat behind. Every angle, every twist she turns he turns with her and at every turn gains ground. If she surrenders or is overtaken does not matter now. She drops into the cover of the salt grass and the hawk falls on her like a stone.

Feathers explode above them, a burst pillow. Before they settle the Coop emerges from the reeds. The mourning dove lies limp-winged, fast in his talons; and he is out of sight, across the river and into the trees.

Most of the time the hunter misses. You could disclaim the panic except, there are so many birds of prey. A hawk or falcon perched above—or standing in—a pile of feathers is a common occurrence. Nothing hereabout dies of old age.

In this way, the excess of the mourning doves goes to good purpose, conjoining penance, forgiveness, and greed. If that is foreign to us, this perfect unity, perhaps it is because the risk we face is self-inflicted. Alone in Creation it kills, but does not eat.

Father's Day

When I was four, just after we'd moved and when for the first time I had a room of my own, my father took me down the street to get a haircut. This too was a first or at least, it is the first haircut I can remember that was just my father, and me. The barbershop had a gumball machine studded with prizes. It stood at head height, impossible to ignore. I asked my father for a penny and told him I wanted one of the miniature pocketknives, and he explained that I couldn't count on getting what I wanted, that there was an element of chance, but he gave me the penny anyway.

I understood what he meant. But I also knew in that

instant, chance had nothing to do with it. It was *certain*.
I could feel it. I dropped in the coin, turned the handle,
and a pocketknife with a single blade inside its brown
plastic case of imitation bone dropped into the slot. I
picked it out and handed it to him so he could see it and
he handed it back. It was clear to me that my father was
happy because I was happy, and because it was the first
piece of luck we'd ever shared, and perhaps because I as-
sumed he was surprised (which I was not), I owed him
an explanation.

"Do you want to know how I did it?" I asked. He said
he did. Even then I knew what I was about to say was
strange and I made him promise not to tell anyone. He
promised. I thought about it for a moment, and unable to
express what had happened in any other way I said, "I
think to God."

Later, I heard him sharing the story with my mother.
I was absolutely humiliated. It was a long time before
that sense, that knowing asserted itself again.

I was living in New York when I got the call, long
feared, that my father would not live through the night.
On the train to Boston, I woke just before dawn and looked
out the window. Directly overhead a perfect quarter-
moon hung in the sky like an empty bowl, and I wondered
if it was a sign of my father's passing. It was exactly 5:57,
and my father, I later learned, had just died.

New Year's Day of 2000 would have been my father's
eighty-fifth birthday. A few days before, my wife Valerie

and I had been talking about owls and the discussion turned to how the owl represents the soul. We had been hearing a great horned owl, rarely, over the course of the Fall and I began thinking how much I wanted to hear him again. That very morning, first day of the Millennium, at exactly 5:57 AM he obliged me. And I thought, Okay, if you *really* want to show me something, show me the owl. At dusk, in the very last light of that day an enormous great horned owl landed on the dead cedar at the edge of the salt marsh not fifty feet from our windows. He looked at us. Then he flew away.

My father once told me he would love me his whole life, and even after. I think he was telling the truth.

SUMMER

Listen to the Mockingbird

There is nothing mawkish about the Mockingbird. Though he mimics many dialects (*Mimus polyglottos*) he is sincere in what he has to say if less than *logikos* (sane). For he has no fear of me, or of the dog next door, or even the cat who lurks beside the backyard fence and watches while he balances, half on, half off the deck chair as he sings of things I know not of, such as what he sees from the tops of the trees (*ti omorfos thea!*), his own beautiful view.

Every day he visits. Only berries and insects need fear him. True (*alithinos*), his wife will lay her eggs in some other bird's nest and leave them there. Consider them guests, travelers on the way who impart as much as they

take. And what a symphony their children make! Would
you have it any other way? *Ochi* (no).

The Mockingbird is like a sponge. All things are his
Muse (*Mousa*), and every bird that ever sang he borrows
from. No mother, no father taught him their trills, these
burrs and churrs and lilting words. That synthesis is all his
own. And he sings at dawn and he sings at dusk and
throughout the day, sometimes only muttering to himself
as if to say "And so forth, and so on (*kathexis*)." Thus begs
the question: What's in a word (*morfima*)? Do we need to
know each and every particle of speech to understand
him? *Siga-siga* (little by little), I think I do. I've come to
believe that his idea (*idea*) of happiness or even bliss is not
dissimilar to our own—except—that he leads a simplified
life and likes it. *Oti, tha ithela* (Me too).

Not everyone appreciates the Mockingbird. He has
his detractors. Sometimes a mourning dove or a cardinal
will come to join the *chorodia* (chorus), captured by his
many voices only to dismiss as gibberish the *Sophia* (Wis-
dom) that he offers. To them this caution: Not so glib. For
if Babel is a parable then Mockingbird has writ its opposite. His ramblings point to a greater truth: We all live
under just one roof and when it comes to laughter, pleasure, pain, we speak the same language (*omoglossos*), all of
us. And if what he has to tell us seems foreign as *Ellinikos,*
the language of the Greeks, perhaps like him we should
learn to speak at least one of the Mother Tongues that ours
comes from.

Snow in Summer

Snowy Egret lands, the name and color of a substance she will never see. There on the muddy bank, still as chalk her carved and ancient figure stands, stilting. Like Nike she leaps sailing into the bright, wide-winged above the shallow water where she feeds, so white sunlight seems shadow.

What could be the purpose of such brilliance, Snow in Summer? Perhaps in some prior life this most strident, most absolute of colors kept her safe. Perhaps she lay to in a frigid land and all these amazing feathers are only artifact of dim ice ages past. Or in the brief season between her comings and goings this is her temporary color, as polished and transparent as paper made of rice. Except, there is no other phase than white in egret-painted skies.

There is fragility in all this. The bird, the salt marsh where she lands, even the turbulent sand. From the South the assault comes by hurricane, each season earlier and more ferocious than the last. From the North it is the melting. And where there is no flood, drought. There is no reprieve. As the brackish plain is silted out or altogether gives way, where will Snowy Egret go? How will she retreat from Winter when Winter itself is in retreat?

When the sun pounds like the hammer to the anvil all life is forged to the blow. The upper latitudes break away. The equator burns. North and north and north the southern creatures go driven there by unfamiliar weathers. Life once rare becomes common. The common vanishes. Perhaps it is not camouflage but survival of a more intense and personal kind that turns the egret white, reflecting not just light, but heat. Maybe she will be all right. What about us, I wonder.

Eye of the Beholder

Among all herons only one is the color of smoke. In a room full of powerful and famous men tamping pipes and puffing cigars, they'd never notice Little Blue. Even if they did they would dismiss him as scant collateral to the prime purpose of marsh and wood. Which purpose, to the roar of handmade guns, is to take aim at partridges with their wings clipped, quail released on cue like pigeons made of clay except that pottery doesn't flutter. No sport to shoot what does not bleed.

Shoot rather than *Hunt* because hunting requires a minimum of one risk out of two:

a. The hunted has at least a chance to get away.

- Or -

b. What is hunted is also hunting *you*.

To argue for your life with a lion like a Maasai, nothing in your fists but a lion spike (the sharp flame-hardened scapula of a giraffe) which you thrust, bare-handed, into the lion's maw impaling him as he bites down and mauls you with his outstretched paws—now that is hunting.

Meanwhile, Little Blue hones his own silent weapons. One of beak. One of eye. Beak jabs its blue-gray length pointy as a knitting needle obliquely into water, returning every third or fourth or fifth time with a meal pincered crosswise like a stitch. For a moment the little fish is suspended as if the heron must consider before he eats. The inquiry is brief. None escape once examined by Little Blue. The other weapon is his eye and in fact it is this that matters first, and most. All Seeing, as if polarized it penetrates the crinkled surface down through the moiré and chiaroscuro of moving water. Or if the water is smooth and hard as a mirror made of silver, still it pries into the deeps. The shimmerings of scales, the dart of shadow, the thin corkscrew-turbulence left by fins, all things are revealed.

Little Blue blinks just once before he strikes and even then he is always watching. A nictitating membrane, that semilucent second lid protects him from what lurks beneath when his head plunges in. Through this golden diver's goggle he keeps his prey in sight till his neck springs back, upright, water flicking away like jewels and the gemmy fish fast in its fate. It was a fair fight after all.

Full but not replete, Little Blue Heron takes to the sky. A single "RaaNH!" announces his departure. He flies, gray form on gray skies, away to where he sleeps and dreams. In the middle of the night that guttural call comes all of a sudden sounding, an annunciation of imagined flight. Unlike us, his dreams come true.

Lachrymae

In the dark the owl swoops unseen down at the speed of death. A feather clipped by a branch from his powerful wing drifts, and twirls, and lands where I will find it when day breaks. In the long-shadowed afternoon the killdeer cries, "Go 'way, go 'way!" and when I won't she does, but leaves the smallest trace of herself behind, quill of the pen for a miniature hand, white and black and brown. The willet and her mate, buttressed against my trespass, have done the same.

I have an antique jar, the glass iridescent with age in which I keep these feathers and the others I have found, collected the way the Romans gathered tears.

There is an egret feather, light as a snowflake.

This one the blue jay gave me, bright as a jewel.

These in their different stripes were gifts from human friends, one of a red-tailed hawk passing inches from the giver's face, three from a parrot that lives in Northern Australia, caught, unlucky, by the only outdoor cat between Cahills Crossing and the Arafura Sea.

This one, blooming with color like a flower? A yellow-shafted flicker who glanced off the windshield and flew away. When they are young and do not know better they often die that way, crashing against the blurred frame of a speeding car, or headlong toward the windowpane.

I have one from an osprey, a fine dark blade.

Another from a crow, sturdy and compact as the creature who created it.

The red is from a cardinal's tail when the goshawk got him, almost.

I have never found the gray of great blue heron, nor the green-tinged brown of glossy ibis, nor the fine ruby plumes of a hummingbird and perhaps I never will.

The birds who left these calling cards are gone. These feathers were the telltale of their lives. When I run out of room I will pour one out. Will it flutter to the ground or will wind and weather carry it away like tears in rain?

At the Turn of the Tide

In the grainy dusk terns gather and cry. Their voices ring, raspy as the rip of the tide that calls them here. So small they are, their wings almost blue in the turbulent reflections from beneath, the humid light of the sky. In close formation they follow each other. The orange beacon of feet and beak almost gray as day recedes. Only the black cape, draped across the head from nape to eyes, stands out. Proof against glare, it is useless now as the sun tumbles into the sea. The terns will peel off one by one to follow the sun except they will not fall, they storm.

Four grouped together work a ruffled patch of water.

Like Magic Lantern slides, each in a different frame they hover—wings out, wings forward, wings curled like a wave, wings back, and around. Tails spread and wavering they drop their heads, each beak a pointer aiming through a turbulence thick as lava, nor can you penetrate the darkness of their eyes as all absorbs there, a sponge for light. Below, confined by the collision of inrushing waters the bait fish feed flashing their silvery sides, not knowing every flick of a fin, every fleck of a tail is seen, and the terns dive!

In the way of men leaping the rail of a listing liner, wings raised high and together above their heads, they plunge, feet first. A volcano of white rises where they strike, and vanish, swallowed by the deep. A long moment, and another. Doubt closes like a gorget when, skipping and dancing and running each atop his own bubbling wake as if it is the easiest thing, the terns one by one come resurrected into air.

As suddenly as they appeared they are gone. Even their voices have left us. The rusting channel markers bob in the slack. Only quiet rules where all this life and death was rhyming only a clock tick past. Some of the terns have eaten their fill. Others having filled their crops leave with two and three plump bait held sideways in their mouths in trust for other mouths whose hunger must be fed, if this fragile existence is to carry on. This time it was the fish who paid, a Roman retribution, Decimation, the taking of every tenth man. But the dawn will come when a tern does not dive but pinwheels into the sea and his essences return to become once more, the little fishes.

How proud the fisherbird in the catch and cull. How certain in his Fate.

Cleanliness

Gulls gather after the storm. Fresh water is a boon to them, puddles their reward for having survived the unseasonable violence of the weather. Preening and primping beyond the needful bounds of cleanliness they splash and dip for the sheer joy of it, bowing their heads again and again and dunking under, and the washing of the one seems to encourage the washing of the others.

Great Egret moves in impossible ways, performing the task she must, every day. Craning her long neck into the characters of some foreign alphabet even she cannot read she reaches every where. Down to the root she goes, each feather stropped and straightened. Though she performs this task for herself alone, she takes her time; there is no part of her that does not shine.

Nearby, Redwing bathes on a hammock of sedges. The vaguely brackish water there is the best he can do. He cannot linger. He has left his guard post above the nest only for the necessity of quenching thirst. Beyond this, the few quick splashes are a luxury and all he has time for. Beads of water fling away from him like pearls. What he lacks in time he makes up in vigor.

When the pool dries out, even then it continues to serve its purpose. The dust that remains has a special value. Animals as large as elephant, as small as a swallow bathe in dust, in dust the things that bite are done in. Antipodes of Antaeus, touching Earth does them no good. But I think the birds, fluttering there in the powdery clay would prefer water if they had a choice, and the elephants if they can, spend twenty in the wet for every single minute in the dry.

Rat in his boneless skittering skin glides across the subway tracks, up one steel rail, down the other, now in between the ties. The underground is filthy with grease, inherently foul, yet Rat's fur glistens clean as a rich woman's cloak. His feet are pink, his eyes are black but full and bright as a bird's despite the lack of light or of a view. He lives well in this subterranean domain unlike his human counterparts, unclean because no one touches them at all.

The closest most animals come to touch is like the communal bathing of the gulls, where touch is only with the eyes. In bathing, their foremost urge is to be clean and the closeness mostly artifact. Here we diverge. From the time when human beings were covered in fur and spoke in gutturals and purrs, before we ventured on two legs, we groomed each other. To be clean required at least two; And from this came our need for caresses. Only our close relations—orangs, chimps and the gorillas, the monkeys and baboons—continue that practice now. Gaining language, losing that natural coat and its necessities, clean and close are no longer intimates and we must make an extra effort to be more than only clean.

The Sanitation Workers' Union Is Happy to Serve You

Through the treetops the vulture looks small. It is not true. She is huge. Open-mouthed, intent on the ground below, she glides without effort. Wind whispers on her dark unruffled wings. Even the feathers barely move. Wheeling, too slow, like a lost kite she is carried on and away . . .

The vulture is a turkey vulture. First broom of the morning collection crew she is stark in her duties, immune to the world in every sense. Carrion does not offend because the smell is sweet to her. Putrefaction cannot harm her nor what the dead harbor within whether large, or small, or invisible. And despite her work she herself is remarkably clean. Clean, inside and out. We recoil at the sight of her though left to her own devices she harms no living being. Quite the contrary. Without her and those of her kind, life would become impossible and the world entire a charnel house. Hers is a profession, true and honorable and perhaps (our lurid fantasies notwithstanding) Nature's oldest.

The disposal of what trundles off the stage has always been an integer of existence. It begins with the Archaea, small and most ancient, and travels Evolution's branches right to our back door. Our ancestors stole the remains of what others had left uneaten long before we learned to hunt for ourselves and for a good while after. Oh yes, that was us, scrambling away from the saber-toothed cat returned ferocious to the kill, competing for scraps with jackal and hyena, with rat and eagle—and vulture.

On the bare granite of an outer island two greater black backed-gulls are having a private feast. They share without rancor something red and ragged which appears at first glance to be a crab, but is not. Crabs do not have wings, do not creep on webbed orange feet. One black duck will never fly again, the deep rose madder of flight muscles engorged with heme and power, all useless to her now. She feels no pain. Her wings when the gulls turn her over are dull as jet and the blaze at her shoulder, an iridescent violet in life, in death is a streak of gray. How she came to this final impasse is an open question.

Her feathers seem intact, no indication of old age or disease. Perhaps startled in the dark there was a collision, or a wrong landing; though her bill is not broken it is hard to say about the rest of her. Whether the black-backs found her already dead or were the ultimate agency is equally unknowable.

Alone among scavengers, turkey vultures almost never kill. They have no need. As long as there is Life, Death itself provides. In this they offend Immortality and Profit and most of us would not miss them. But when the vultures are gone, what true monsters will come home to roost?

Food for Thought

The ruby-throated hummingbird weighs less than four grams and fits in a gently closed hand with room enough to come to no harm. Inside the hollow of its skull is a brain smaller than a large seed yet serves every need of a creature who—can fly point to point for one quarter the earth's circumference with no map, hover in place forwards and back on wings beating fifty times a second, hear sound as slow as two cycles (twenty times better than you and me) and thereby in theory recognize the thundering of the sea from a thousand miles away, and navigate by this also.

Ruby-throat migration begins in spring in Costa Rica

and continues all the way to Canada. Some head inland by routes unknown. Some follow the coast all the way to Maine. Others fly across the Gulf of Mexico in one straight shot because, once over water, there is no place of stopping. All this they sustain by simple sugars in the nectar of flowers and by the insects on which they feed. Very small insects. For this reason insecticide is an enemy, and herbicides because they destroy the wildflowers we sometimes call weeds. And housecats. And window glass. The only danger not man-made is cold, and though this too can be deadly they've evolved to cope with that.

Baring calamity, female ruby-throated hummingbirds live almost a decade. The males whose iridescent crimson throats give the species its name don't fare as well. Though they do not war, they posture as if they might: Even the pitch of their hum changes, the quotidian hummingbird roar, chasing all comers from the vicinity of food and mate and nest. It costs them. The threat of violence takes energy and time and wears them down, contributing to an earlier demise.

The best way to bring hummingbirds into your garden is by what you plant. Red, trumpet-shaped flowers are the ones they prefer. Columbine, bee balm, red honeysuckle, and just to test the rule, yellow jewelweed, the off-white of milkweed, and butterflyweed in bright orange. All are New England natives and hummingbirds love them, and will remember where they found them year after year. If you want to make a human memory, take a child by the hand and stand quietly in the midst of blossoms. Hummingbirds when they come will largely ignore you, feeding within inches, humming that song to which only they know the words though the child will never forget the tune.

The deepest connection to hummingbirds that I know of is beyond peace or violence, recollection or forgetfulness, or words. The poet e.e. cummings told Charles Norman, his biographer, that the hummingbirds at cummings's feeder would bow their good-bye to him before their long journey south. I don't think Norman believed him. But on the morning of September 2, 1962, they were sitting on the screen porch of cummings's New Hampshire farmhouse when two ruby-throats appeared. "Like the tiniest helicopters," Norman wrote, "the hummingbirds rose straight up to the top of the screen, then descended, five or six times, then were gone."

That afternoon cummings died. I like to think he went with them.

The Kingfisher

Kingfisher flies from the bend in the river to the edge of the marsh, lord of all he sees. He stays awhile and then continues on his rounds like the squire he conceives himself to be. Now straight as a shooting star he heads out to the beach and perches there about the middle of his range. Watching the water below that is rippled with wind somehow, through all that turbulence he finds the little fishes and, diving in, returns with a silvery minnow dangling from his beak. And he does that almost every time.

Kingfisher shuns bold water. Look for him beside the river; in the lee of the long outer barrier; inshore atop the spiles of a narrow groin. Sequestered, he is safe from where the ocean rolls unobstructed, safe from what lies beyond where even Kingfisher can see. Every day just before the day arrives, before the sky turns violet to blue, there in his one place or the other you will hear Kingfisher chattering. That call, which says "All this is *Mine*," is familiar to everyone who lives near to the salt marsh or the sea, as is the way he hovers, and the particular flutter of his wings, Flap-flap glide, Flap-flap-flap glide. Any of these will tell him even at a distance, but though many birds are intermittent in flight and there are more than a few who hover, none can duplicate his call. "D'D'D'DON'T!" he cries, every annoyance met this way, animal or human, alive or elemental. Even the rising globe of the sun, too bright, makes him raise his voice.

Solitary autocrat, it never occurs to Kingfisher that anyone has rights here but himself. In this he is a charmer, his hubris the thing that endears. For it is after all only a small space that he defends, only a little country. Green Heron will stand in Kingfisher's place and cover that same expanse in four deep wing beats thinking that territory also his territory. Kingfisher does not agree and Green Heron will not challenge him and flees. The same discretion is not to be expected from hawks or falcons and I have seen Merlin, talons out, shooting the riverbed in deadly pursuit, Kingfisher screaming, the falcon unrelenting.

I do not know how that one ended and do not want to know. Kingfisher lives as if he will live forever. Let him.

Pied Pipette

Greater Yellowlegs sashays along the narrow channel with a name only half true. Though her legs are as colorful as a crayon, to call them Great is at best an inaccuracy and at most, hubris. Diminutive and dainty and delicate are the better words for her; timid is not one of them. Close and above and in plain view we are of no concern. Only the ragged stitch of waterway guides her, and only the tide behind will force her to go.

Among the ruined sea lavender waiting to be reborn and the sedge come again to greening she tiptoes almost creeping. Hardly a ripple she makes. There is no wind. The mottling that is her camouflage half hides, while those legs flash like a beacon and give her away. Their probable purpose is to serve notice to others of her kind that it is she who comes, perhaps searching out a mate. But not today. Today she is by herself, with nothing in her bearing to suggest she would have it any other way.

A self-assurance belied by tiny size should shout for numbers and the comfort and protection of a crowd, out loud. It doesn't. Nor does she wear her loneliness like a shroud. There is no cosmic misery in her calm face. No tension there. No undue crying out though she is known for her piercing cry. Only, gently softly does she go, self-assured as a demidivine, some lesser deity of salt marsh and the low-lying part of the sky. She brags no further aspirations. No pretense nor interpretation beyond *This Is,* and *I am,* and it can be no otherwise.

Unlike the wading hunters, the herons and others who share this grand greengrassed marshland, she does not stab or pluck or crush and tear. Tiny tiny are the things she consumes there and she does this in a most remarkable way. Her long bill, open just this much (not more) exploits a fact of nature: Water of its own accord will rise on the sides of a straw—or the long phalaropean bill of Yellowlegs feeding. Narrowing that strawlike bill, a drop of water will move upward. Open; now repeat; and you have a pump. When Yellowlegs seems to clap her bill quick as a cat lapping milk she is taking sustenance.

Animals too small to see ride down her throat while the excess water rushes out.

Greater Yellowlegs lip-smacking, is it a sign of satisfaction or indifference to the way things taste? I only know in Nature nothing goes to waste.

The Weaver of Sleep

Knit one pearl two, Orb Weaver stitch stitch stitches the names of the guests who will come to visit her. She is patient. She is kind. She welcomes without limit, without fear, all who enter her neatly kept abode. No waiting at the desk in vain, ringing the bell for the bell-boy who will not come. She carries you bag and baggage on her own, as heavy or light as you may be, right to your room. She lays you down and tucks you up in a quilt wound of the finest stuff, all snug and warm. And dims the light. And shuts the door.

This is no ordinary bed and breakfast. Not an old and mossy inn, the creaking step, the broken hinge, the screen door. Think Tall. Think Grand! This construct, scraping high and wide against the nighttime sky, would she not call herself a builder? Magnificent as any bridge, cabled and anchored and buttressed against impact and wind shear and the accumulated weight of rain, stronger than any suspension you can name, each strand, twice the strength of steel all made by hand.

Or is it cord, not alloy that she draws through the plate, that silvery gift spread upon the floor, a carpet of exotic name? Kilim? Kurd? Baluch? An ancient geometric copied from the court of Minos, the tombs of Kriti? But then, where is the loom? No treadle or warp beam, no shuttle except herself, round and round and round as the circles of her weft are wove. No beater does she pull against the frames. The threads, bonded at the points of her design (however loose or tight the weave) hold fast, and those who enter (though lightly they may tread) discover in the heart a certain dread . . .

At dawn she folds the cloth away, unraveling what was built the night before. Was she unsatisfied, not gratified, or is she bored? Or is frugality her game? Her day for night. Her dark is day. Now privacy she craves and into a nave, a nook, some hidden place retires while outside across the yard others tie their hammocks eight hands wide. The garden spider, gold and black and many times her size, has no fear of things abroad by light. Among the greenery this one embroiders not to welcome but to warn away. That zigzag overlay lettered to the center of every web tells the birds and perhaps the dragonflies to duck and dodge. Others with less perspicacity will luckily recline there, wings undone, one last siesta in the noonday sun.

Toward dusk, with a yawn, Orb Weaver wakes and ties the wires down, by gravity, by strength of arm. See how carefully she balances, Philippe Petit without the bar, Flying Wallendas without an audience; for in the end she is a homebody, the front porch as far as she will venture out, sunset the only footlight that she knows and her only candle is the stars. She casts the net all wet with dew, a Milky Way of silk and she is Mars.

Red, White, and Blue

I have the phone long distance in my left hand and now the camera in the right and my neck is craned to an impossible angle trying to hold onto the one and not drop the other because a dozen feet away is a bird I've never seen though recognize immediately, and as if this were not enough what am I thinking? I'm thinking: *Valerie's going to kill me.*

"You saw this?"

"Uh-huh."

"You just saw this? You took that picture *here*?"

"'Bout three minutes ago."

"I hate you,"(slug on the arm), "I hate you!"

Attorney: Your Honor the respondent deliberately and with malice aforethought saw and photographed an Indigo Bunting—

(Jury: Collective gasp*)*

—whilst his wife was briefly away from the premises.

Me: Yah but—

Attorney: Further, respondent's contention that "Valerie grew up in Reading P.A. and what does she know from birds?" is hardly a defense coming from a man who grew up in the slums of Malden besides which, he saw the bird he photographed the bird and knowing it would cause his wife acute emotional distress nevertheless he showed her the very photo of the bird.

(Quiet weeping from the plaintiff's bench)

Me: Yah but—

Judge: Enough! Decree granted. Valerie gets the house-truck-camera-checkbook, and you? For you gornisht.

In my childhood there were two kinds of wildlife: English sparrows, and pigeons. My grandparents' next-door neighbor had a pigeon coop. He kept offering to give my grandfather a pigeon for me but my grandfather always turned him down. He said they were filthy. He was right. I would have loved it. Meanwhile, every morning he put out stale bread on the rail of the second-story porch just outside the kitchen windows which brought—pigeons.

We watched them eat while my grandmother sang me a song about chickadees, a bird I had never seen. It was an event if in spring you so much as *heard* a robin. I do remember my mother calling me to see a great of flock of geese in V formation heading South. This happened exactly twice in all the time I was growing up. Valerie says she had house finches, but that was after they moved and she was already in her teens. We both had squirrels. The only other animals I ever saw were stray dogs and the neighbor's cat who used to visit until she was hit by a car.

What makes two kids from a world of weeds and asphalt so passionate about the wild, transported, completely, upon a magic carpet of Indigo Bunting?

Indigo is a deep blue that comes from the Indigo plant, used for dyeing inexpensive cloth. Far from the source, where even this was a luxury the cloth was cut in strips, for bunting. Women sewed the bunting to the hems of homespun skirts and the collars of shirts and the cuffs of blouses. Their life was brittle, easily broken. Go to the tombstones, read the dates, read the names: Baby Wheaton; and buried alongside Mary Wheaton, Mother, Died in Childbirth Aged 23; and the empty grave of Randolph, Husband, Father, lost at sea. In the middle of their short hard lives they wiped away the sweat and saw a glimmer of bright blue, saying, "Will you look? Will you look at that! He's just the color of Indigo Bunting..."

This evening there was no sunset. Clouds as dark as battle smoke are rolling in from the West and there is wind.

Snowy egrets, billowing up on pointy wings are bright as
star shells and the cardinals, dulled to the color of dried
blood in this last light come now for a final repast as night
pulls shut the door. And we see the Red, and we see the
White, and we wait for sleep that will not come and think
of Blue as blue as bunting, and spacious skies, and purple
distant peaks, and the inexorable amber crackling of the
lightning that is to come.

FALL

Top Gun

The Birds of Prey have begun their passage. Bottled up by bad weather they wait, and then upon the freshened air, a hurricane of hawks roars through. Goshawk and Broadwing, Roughleg and Redtail, all are here. So are the falcons, Merlin with that Prussian dueling scar across his eye and Thousand-yard Stare. Kestrel, hovering above the marshland all bright feathers, formidable beyond her size. Late this afternoon Peregrine cutting across the shallowing sun, almost transparent in the penetrating light. While all the small that walk that fly that crawl that climb quake with dread.

Predators prey. Prey flees.

This morning we had a Sharp-shin. He too must feed and the songbirds fear this little hawk with reason. He may not succeed every time but he tries, sitting in plain sight on a naked branch while everyone hides.

Except the Jays.

One by one by one Bluejays alight on the fork of the very same tree. A lethal error in judgment seems to lead them close, closer.

Too close.

Blasting from his perch the Sharpy strikes, the spurs of his talons scalpel-sharp, his feet spread like fangs. Twisting, he turns and dives headfirst, half upside down, dogging the nearest Jay a tailfeather's width behind.

The Bluejay, screaming blood and murder, escapes— just barely—and comes right back for more. And more. Each time that blinding terror, each time the narrow escape, each jay taking his turn as if they want to be eaten. Suicide, by hawk! And then I understood: *The bluejays are playing a game.*

When we ride the Cyclone careening toward the bottom at an angle sure to jump those roller-coasting tracks—We scream! We love it. We ride that ride again.

This is how Bluejays play it. Hawk does not but then, not his turf, not his rules. One guess who tired first?

Prey plays, Predators gnash their teeth.

Smart Money's on the Game.

Nostalgia

In the woods a young robin is singing. He lacks the resonance of his elders and his melody is wrong, the voice too high, the phrases broken like a child reciting an anthem he does not yet comprehend. "For Whitchit Stands," he sings, unsure if it is a place or a person and what *does* a Whitchit stand for? Those who might teach the robin have mostly gone south, or if not, class is definitely out. The staff was done with that work months ago. If his memory is vague and his song flawed who can fault him? He hangs on just to keep us company, and to remind us what the season used to be.

The leaves are still green but not for long. We only

await the inevitable. It is cool at night and soon it will be colder, cold enough to regret it, and the time until next heat will be drawn and long. At least, though we are well into October, the waking hours are warm beneath the sun and in any sheltered place it does not feel like Fall, much less the ragged edge of Winter.

Now the cardinal adds her newfound voice, a single stanza strong and complete. She is not confused. She is just practicing. Like the robin she recalls better weathers. Like the robin, some vague memory in bones and blood hearkens, she does not know toward what, only that she and the robin would rather be there. Will soon be there.

So they sing the swans in long lines late in the day, even their wings a warning whistling like wind over ice. And they sing the lowering angle of the sun, closer to horizon than to sky, robin who has yet to feel his first hard frost and cardinal who remembers the season she was born, that northern paradox, chill air, warm light. Like a blanket warding off the night, like a candle lit against the snow, comfort settles upon all things when out of season Red Birds sing.

Big Fish Little Fish

Down-tide from the mouth of the river, spray, arc upon arc, catapults from the sea. Also white against the bright blue comes every gull up and down the bight drawn by the frenzy just off shore. The hunt is on. There is blood in the water. What eats, on top, is driving down through what is eaten. It is pandemonium, it is magnificent, something being torn to pieces and too much excitement to care.

Chances are it's bonito running the coast, closing for the slaughter. Strategic. Efficient. Theirs is a well-articulated mayhem, they do their work abruptly and depart. The gulls taking their bit with them are already away.

It is not a reprieve. It is a lull.

Again the water boils with the cut and swirl of fins and at once there are bunker right up on the beach. Flopping and thrashing they roil the receding waves in a panic so deep they would rather drown, here, in thin air, than brave whatever it is, down there. If they remain they will die. If they return they will die. Mouths agape, gills pumping emptiness they stay, longer than they can and longer still and only when it seems impossible do they writhe and wriggle their way back in.

It will not save them.

Drawn by carnage, or instinct, or some uncanny knowledge of where and when to try his luck, a single osprey comes. Powering down the line he stalls, hovering, then plummets into the surf. Instead of rising he sits shoulder-deep in the shallow, wings stretched all the way out like a pair of arms as if relaxing in the biggest bathtub in the world; while, unseen, his talons do their terrible magic. At last two strong wing beats and up he comes, a bunker dangling beneath like Antaeus strangled in air, a certain death but slow.

So Big Fish eats Little Fish and is eaten, and nothing born that does not kill to survive.

Tintinnabulation

On the flyout the tree swallows rise with a roar. Up and up and up and fold into a single form, then spread then crash then break apart and drop down low, just above the island's shore. Five hundred thousand pairs of wings beat five hundred thousand muted bells, and toll left, and toll right, and dive into the tall reeds and disappear: No sign; No sound; Not come to rest but a vanishing. Consumed. Then spit out, chord by phrase by crescendo, an echo of birds, dark and brilliant notes upon the sky.

Allegretto. The cloud of swallows rolls and lofts, a C above high C, clarion to passing hawks and falcons. How it turns their predatory ears and eyes. Passing through and through this great music whose instrument is the living flesh of birds their talent fails them; they depart, hungry and worn out.

Finale. In the last descent the swallows funnel down, a grand cacophony. Here they feel most vulnerable, each phrase *tutto presto* as speed replaces virtuosity. But nothing can follow them, can capture more than a blur. Wings folded back like sixteenth notes cascading in slurs and in staccato, only a shiver marks their entrance into the phragmites, a fall that should have broken bones. Perhaps, like the conductor's stern baton—abruptly pianissimo—it is the reeds themselves that bring them to a stop and this safe cushion is why they come here, for the coda of soft landing. To sleep. To wait. To arise once more . . .

Daybreak. Tree swallows go their separate ways. They will stop for bayberry when they can find it but mostly they will feed on insects plump with the indulgences of Summer and the mild days of early Fall. Over water they gather the all-but-invisible life that hovers there, scooping with open mouths and tiny tongues.

The Connecticut is an ancient parchment, its ebb and flow a score long studied and well known. Winter is the great river's last movement, a measure tree swallows can never master, a chorus they must not sing on pain of death. Though their rounded bodies attest to the syntony, acclaim will therefore be late, sung by tree swallows only at their grand returning to this once and still untrammeled place—

Encore! Encore! Encore . . .

Labor Day

When did America run out of honest work? We used to line up round the block for $2.75 an hour on the clock and glad to get it. Now, I get no vacation no benefits and on their twelve bucks? I can't afford a brown-bag lunch (it's barely a living on twice that much). Meanwhile, to hear Big Business talk, cheap is never cheap enough. But who will do the chores drive the engines sweep the floors when even the (is it Tuvanese?) can't make it on the gruel they proffer. Animal Help Wanted is the last job on offer:

❧

POSITIONS SOUGHT

Elephant—Rural fire departments, save big on gas and equipment too. Self-contained transport, forty-gallon capacity trunk. Will work for ... Do I have to spell it out? NO ladder companies, please!

Lemming—Good leadership qualities. Willing to travel.

Saltwater Croc—Comes with own armor, weapons, BAD attitude. Fully amphibious. Move over Blackwater. When I say I'm gonna eat your lunch ... I mean it!

Twenty-four Blackbirds—Royal bakers. Salary negotiable. Slice of the pie a prerequisite.

Matched Pair of Namibian Lions—Strong. Vigilant. Noble. Building a new library or refurbishing an old one? Picture us on your front stoop.

Striped Bass—58 inches. Available to sport fishermen for the best photo op ever. Sorry, strictly catch and release.

Brown Bat—Highly trained in Organic pest control. I neva meta mosquita I didn't wanna eata. Night shift preferred.

HELP WANTED

Leeches—Unique business opportunity. Call our Collections Department during normal banking hours.

As the Crow Flies—Explorers need guide to most direct route west. Ask for Mr. Lewis, or Mr. Clark.

Ursa Major—Wall Street firm of excellent standing seeks
   Bear to work for *other* Wall Street firm of excellent
   standing. References provided. *Don't* tell them who
   sent you.

Decorator Crab—Must have good color sense. Send
   swatches. Ask for M. Stewart, CEO. It's a good thing.

Poet Seeking Inspiration—River, Sunset, Hawk-eyed
   Hawk on fire, Dab-stabbing Heron, etc. Contact Mr.
   Thomas, Wales (the place not Leviathan).

Pack Rat—National archives needs experienced cura-
   tor. Hereditary position. Make yourself at home.

Owls—Messenger. Apply Parthenon. Ask for Athena.

R. U. Ready for your Close-up?—Seeking wildlife of
   every size genus and encryption for inspiration and
   description thereof. Some late-lingering Great Egret
   white as the snows that are to come might be the
   perfect one. No need to call ahead, just show up.

The Rout

The sea rolls in like a screen door shuffling in the wind. The tide is low. A small sloop has shipped its keel on the bar. Its jib, come loose at the leech, is in tatters. The slap of the cloth sounds like applause though the cove is empty and the boat stands alone. The integument of Summer has been broken, a seedpod ruptured by an angle of the light. And out of the bright Osprey comes.

He is young. You can tell by the body's heft, the breadth of the back, a head not fully plumed in that grizzled white of majority. Not wizened, not yet wise. And how he tries.

Dive! A fall to break bones—straight in—then out

and up and water shedding like rain, his talons empty. He circles round powering without economy and again—straight in—and fails—and dives and not quite and dives and almost and climbs an oarsman who's shot his slide, all akimbo, and on his face The Fear. The wide eye. The wild way he wings above the beach. The tension of his shoulders on the downbeat. Each entry becomes an act of will. Each near miss a curse. Muscles burn. Strength consumed. All sight all senses focused on the prize as once more into the surf he flies.

Luck! Up from the brine the spume the clawing wave he pulls, blooded by the fish underneath his wings. Only three talons out of four, only one foot out of two holds fast but that fish is forward-looking (So!), and the grip is through-and-through (True!) and he makes the turn toward land one last time (Home Free!).

Not quite.

Black-backed Gull comes coursing down the bite, his head roving right and left. Larger by inches, heavier by pounds, his cry is terrible. His mouth a steel shear. And he draws near. He too is young and hungry and knows his business in a way Osprey does not. There is no blame in it: Does the Lord not also have Other Mouths to feed? But Osprey is not Job of the Book and will have none of that. His is the right if not the might.

And the oars that are Osprey's wings are fast in their locks now. And he will pull with the beat of a quinquereme away, away, and South'ard. No detour, no other choice, he will keep this fish to live and fish once more.

It is good, for Osprey is alone now, his parents departed from the place of his birthing months before. Though they live he is an orphan as we will all be orphans or are orphaned. And all that we have learned and been taught and all that we have triumphed on our own or not can never change it. To Osprey then, in his young and desperate life Good Speed, Be Comforted. Meet Every Need. With no guide except the Truth of North enshrined in the corpus of his brain in particles of magnetite, the mother Lodestone, thus will he find his own way: *Benedicite.*

A Mood in the Weather

A ragtag of stems and leaves shoulders between the cultivars, a homeless man bellying up to the bar. It does not belong there. Coarse, unkempt in the way it grows, a tangle for a crown, if the owner of this ground—manicured now within an inch of its life—if the owner finds it, *zik!* One slash of the pruning knife and it will go the way of all the others. That thicket, full of natives cut away and all the wildlife that traveled there and lived there, fodder of great horned owls, cover of foxes, birthing place of fawns, bramble of wild raspberries sweeter than any market proffers and not at any price—everything—leveled bulldozed banished and only the brushpile grows. Even the young beech tree with its golden leaves clinging as if they think they are not yet dead, sacrificed. That they came here these good people for a piece of the country, for its wilds, for the secret place and then unthinking made the land clean. All except this solitary green survivor, this escapee. Such a terrible compunction to be neat.

But if the plant knows it doesn't show it. It does not bow. Does not wilt. Only bends if there is wind. Though it too will wither and fall away that will not happen yet, not quietly, not without purpose: To her who only waits, All Things Come.

Inflorescences bursting from her every joint and bract gleam with the Color of Kings. No matter. You notice them last. Not the late optics of rod and cone but the provinces of our remnant reptilian brain turn the head. Toward the flittering; the fluttering; the clicking wings of butterflies.

That an ancient part of us revives is right as these insect forms are very ancient also, an Origami folded and cut tens of millions of years before the evolution of the hand, *autodidaktos*. And if we are drawn by motion the life that alights is drawn by hue alone and the textures and patterns in which it is revealed. Without the flower and that miraculous capacity to notice at a distance the butterfly does not exist. True, single molecules detected far away are the lure. But if Scent is the Long Range Navigation, beacon to the insect world, then the Flower is both landing lights and the object of the flight: Inside nectar hides, plentiful and sweet.

Five kinds of lepidoptera converge at the purple aster. They are distinct as elements. Hues of earthen yellow and blue metal, water green and the violet of air, the dusty brown of wood, paint the prized illuminations of their wings. What fantasy. Eyes where no eyes exist, to frighten and confuse. Pure transparencies, the only windowpane in Nature. Swirls and iridescences elaborate as sunrise. All this on just one side, as the underleaf is often not the same.

An American Lady unfurls her impossible tongue and drinks, wings gently pulsing. She needs every drop. The hour is very late for her. Most of her exotic pigment and moiré has been lost to wear and tear and every edge is ragged, worn out, those wings which are her last and only pair. I wonder if she knows these days of golden light are coming to an end, and whether the intensity is desperation or the absolute of the way she chose to live. Beside her a Yellow Sulphur lands, and then another American Lady, the younger brighter mirror of her self. It is a mirror she chooses not to share. The old girl lifts and goes to the next and a Hoary Edge takes her place. Then a Cabbage butterfly. Only the Monarch stands apart. As if he has abandoned his prerogatives, all day he has ignored the purple aster seeking only flowers that are white, fresh confessions of mortality.

First frost. The asters are brown except for one, its

petals dried to a mauve that is almost pink, a lipstick kiss upon the cup. Nearby and alone the Mantis sits more in contemplation than in prayer, an Incan priest who has run out of hearts.

When Animals Vote

The election they said, was too close to call. Pundits, Pashas, and Prognosticators having all had their say, I decided to do some divining of my own. After voting on this crisp fall morning, notebook in hand I took a short walk to the salt marsh to take an exit poll.

In the politics of Nature you can sort the politically active from the merely vociferous by several well-worn criteria. The geese, collective in flight, alert and organized on the ground are Union members. It is the time of year when the Bosses fire, point-blank, into their noisy demonstrations but there is no keeping the Union down and indeed I did not see a single member. Obviously, they were out politicking. A handful of canvasbacks (the converse of geese) were sitting ducks, they did not vote at all, whereas the rabbits were hopping up and down because they were so anxious to exercise their franchise. Fearing wolves, they said, security was their main concern. I tried to explain that wolves were a poor metaphor. Though much maligned wolves are fairly straightforward creatures who for the most part kill only what they can eat; and that only two or possibly three persons in the entire four hundred years of European settlement of our entire Continent have been killed by wild wolves! What's that got to do with us, asked the rabbits? Point taken I replied. Notwithstanding, rabbits are more at risk from terrors close to home—mosquitoes, ticks, rabid ground squirrels, lightning, for that matter. But the rabbits who (to put it kindly) are not well read later said they voted for the people with the biggest guns—the self-same ones who only days ago were plastering the marsh with goose feathers, as if rabbit fur was bulletproof. Meanwhile, a broad-winged hawk on the tree above my head took flight before I could ask him if he planned to vote and whom he might vote for. I suspect he was an Independent. The sparrows, flitting from branch to branch were apparently undecided. The squirrels, busy packing their larder for the winter, said they would vote the economy. The ants, lockstep, were disappointed in the lack of candidates sufficiently authoritarian but would support the status quo. The mourning doves, in their woe, waited in line in the rain to vote the

alternative slate. The crows, among the smartest creatures, made sure their votes would count by voting early.
The coyotes, stealthy critters, fearful of public places voted
absentee, while the foxes (wanting to write in a winner)
said they would be coming by at dusk, late, and last, when
the outcomes would likely be already known. There was
only one great egret as all the others had gone south to
battleground states and she was much too busy to talk to
the likes of me. Last was an American bald eagle, flying
low and slow along the river. You might expect an eagle
to come down on the side of business, guns, and butter
but he said he was an environmental voter and, having
had his share of combat, antiwar, with little tolerance for
those nearsighted beasts who cannot see the forest for
the trees.

Finally the tally looks like this: Most of the wildlife on
my short list cast their votes on a sense of history, of argu-
ment and reason, and do not regard dissent as treason.

Sum of the Parts

Turk-turk Turkey comes jerk-jerk lurking on, tip to toe. Cautious, like ice just itching to melt. Across parkland, under low-lying limbs drip-drip-dripping with dew. Patient like mud settling where deer, galumphing, stirred up still water. Driving slow and low and through and through from tall grass to scrub. Look at them go. Tough. Bad. Ain't no Butterball, ain't no Song Sparrow. Checking out the quiet part of the woods ahead of would-be girlfriends, might be lovers, always moving cover to cover.

Then right behind taking their sweet time wouldn't you know, here those Birdie-Birds come, tut-stut-strutting their stuff, proud and tall and don't gonna be no one's stuffin'! They might *look* sweet. First best think on this: Before you get to the eats have to beat down twenty pounds of lean, mean muscle armored like a weaponeer. Got spurs on the backs of their legs sharp as a thorn. Got a beak that means business. Fly straight up, chase Someone down the block, wreck SOMEONE'S whoooole day. So back *away*. Keep on lickin' your lips, that "Someone" gonna be YOU!

Morning catches the sheen, at shoulders, back, cusp of wing, iridescent as Mother of Pearl but these ain't no Pretty-pretty Peacocks, no Birds of Paradise makin' nice . . . Don't be calling these turkeys "Turkey" to their face. Feathers broad and flat as dragon scutes, breath like Mace. Neck like a reptile, long and ropey. Glaring; Staring; Violet-blue and Crimson-red. Horn of flesh in the center of the head. Bald as a vulture. Eye as dark as obsidian glass. Feet that leave a four inch track. Pickin' their toes with a clickety-clack!

Like those who have risen from the sea and crawled back in (seal and sea lion, whale and dolphin) some take to the sky only to return to land: Wild Turkey, that Jabberwock, weighty presence, work of art.

Less than the sum, more than the parts.

The Hammer

Tiny as tiny a thing could fly Downy Woodpecker
drops from the sky, and clings. The stem grasped by
his thorny feet is the girth of a tree, its seedpods monu-
mental fruit, such is the scale of things. He cocks his
head. Is he listening? Turning, he shifts from eye to eye.
Is it something that he sees? He drops the angle of his
brow as if sampling some invisible scent upon the wind.
In truth, the needle-piercings of his nostrils do not flare.
With no particular sense of smell there is no need. Pre-
carious, yet he remains secure, in knowledge of how the
job is done and where it lies. And how the chips fly!

There are two dangers equal to all the members of

this tribe. A woodpecker's bill slams into the wood so hard and so-many-times-a-second his brain must be tightly held within the skull against a cumulative lethality. Like a boxer pummeled too many times? The same. The other risk is completely obvious. Like a machinist at the lathe who must protect his eyes? And here too Evolution provides. The nictitating membrane, that tough translucent shield drops over the delicate cornea at every risk of sharp and imminent harm. True, all his effort produces hardly anything to qualify as splinters, only dust and tiny grains. Yet there is grandeur in his game.

Downy Woodpecker whose tempest fits in a demitasse is a larger presence than he seems. He has no fear of me as I watch not ten feet away. He knows his work is to find his work and do it. And so he does: There! The grub, pumpkin yellow, fat as cracklings, tweezed in that agile beak and tasted by the tip of a featherpoint tongue: Yes! Tossed back. Then swallowed. With hardly a pause begins again and quickly finds another. How does he know?

Nobody knows how he knows.

That "He" is more than a figure of speech. The red cockade gives his gender. Peculiar as this may seem, in most of the country so does a preference for narrow stocks and stems, a known male trait. If you hear a Downy high up in the small branches, or low on weed or sapling—chances are it's a boy!

Downy Woodpecker dap-taps his way through the

bounty of this perfect larder. The day may be hard but winter will be harder. Here is the craftsman sure in his trade. He does his job, better than the bossy English sparrows chipping seed at the feeder in their lazy way, better than the mourning doves grown so fat, their fate will be sealed in the talons of hawks and owls. Downy Woodpecker? He's chosen better: To be the hammer, not the anvil.

No (R)Egrets

Garland on the Belt of Venus, Great Egrets glide. The glow behind edges them in shadow while from the other side the low sun taints them bright. Down, and down they drift so slow, alighting in the tops of the trees. They balance on thin branches there, stilt-walkers, grafted to this unlikely place, a place that suits them perfectly. From that high perch they survey all the land, the marshes tinted gold and tinder brown, the painted leaves kiting away. They turn their heads toward sounds others cannot hear, toward movement others cannot see. Inclining their long white necks they capture some incomprehensible thing, a presence only they can feel. Or an absence.

The salt marsh is indeed empty. The sojourn of Summer is over. The wavy water lies unrippled by the stiff-jointed plunk and plack of long-legged feet, unsounded by the stab-dabbling beak, liberator of hapless crabs and little fishes. All the transient cousins have departed save only them, first to arrive in early Spring, last to decamp in Fall and even then, not until the stars are pinpoint and frost has bit the bite of winter. It won't be long. But for now here they stand, swaying, the tropical whiteness of their feathers burning in the frigid air, a color tempting snow. Too large, too show.

Balanced between seasons and hours, muttering in soft and guttural tones meant only for each other Great Egrets hold forth. What do they say? There is no science that will tell us. We cannot even guess. It is an impenetrable conversation neither intellect nor empathy can decipher nor can we know the Why or Wherefore of an inner life as alien as Jupiter or Mars.

Ghostly as they came Great Egrets go, the day's last blush aglow on great white wings.

Neither This nor That

The fog unfolds like the thick white beard of God, a refuge and a silence there. It is bright and blurry, muffling sound as much as light, this morning analogue of the dark. It rounds the edges from every thing.

When cool air meets warm land, cloud clings to ground. Or as now, when land is locked and frozen and air is not, moisture also changes state from solution to suspension. Think of it as water turned granular, like sand. As sand turned wet, dust changed into water. Fog is both conflict and its resolution. Fog is uncertain. Fog is the atmosphere of transition.

No predator, airborne or earth bound finds comfort

in the fog. In fog, acuity deserts them. Sight and sound are veiled, blunted. Even scent becomes confused and convoluted. Robbed by the creeping damp they have lost their edge.

And you'd think the prey would make a heyday, would run and revel and rejoice in this gentle moment of reprieve but they do not. Equally deafened, blinded, equally deprived of the ability to judge distance and speed they come only furtively and momentarily, and warily. Rather than abandoning caution they redouble it. The chickadees, so tame they land inches from my moving hand, even they do not come for fear of the fog and the unseen Hunger though for once, because it is unseen, it does not exist. With some tens of millions of years behind them in which they could have changed their minds they will not change them now.

Only the Canadas are unperturbed. Already resolute, their vigilance has no more room to grow. Necks dipping and rising they graze among the flooded marsh grasses, these inheritors of Diplodocus, feeding and standing guard in turn. Alert, alive, at the edge of what is solid and what is not they are watchful against hawk and eagle from above, fox and bobcat in the stealthy plane, snapping turtle from below. So brave.

Soon, rising as the fog rises they will leave this leaden shore, will sail like clipper ships when the stern wind blows, a wind that looks like Spring and bites like Winter. Like sheets carried off the line they go, wings spinning in the wintry air. Flying fast and straight they careen at barely head height, the rusted voices of the geese and the buzzing of their wings like a young girl blowing on a grass blade through cupped hands for the first time and the last time before she learns this is the province of boys. That is how they sound.

Osprey Fishing in Rain

Sometimes distant sometimes close enough it sizzles (hot grease in the pan), lightning strikes frying the sea frying the land. Rain driving sideways turns to hail, pellets like shrapnel. They will hurt you.

Into this Osprey flies.

Hard rain hauls the Fisherbirds toward the sea. Three, now five, now six cruise the coastline where the Shelf is a narrow taper. They blur in the pouring down and the gray on gray of their shadows against a roiling *coperture* of cloud. The storm rings with their cries as they pass each other in challenge and reply, challenge and reply. . . .

To the end of the long jetty The Protector of Fishes

strides in his great black coat and oilers. He stands against the weather unafraid, watching. One by one by one he sees the osprey fail. They fold to the shape of darts and weapon toward the waves. Sometimes they pull up in the nick and sometimes hit square blasting white foam only to climb again into the air, talons empty. Fishes will die. Or they will die. There is no Middle Grounds among these shallows.

Leaning into the wind The Protector of Fishes tugs his woolen watch cap down.

The cap is Navy Blue, and yes, your head gets wet but stays warm. He likes it that way and the cap belonged to his father. He can almost see him there, back at Quonset Point in '41, running toward a burning B-17. This and the cannonade of thunder he feels in his chest remind him of his uncle too, flying close attack, the German 88 that went clean through the top turret and out the canopy again without exploding. He lost the sight in one eye, hardly a scratch of harm for all that blood and madness, the devolution of men throwing stones.

And like a stone Osprey dives.

Rain white as tracers creases Osprey's feathers but this time by blind luck or faculty he finds his mark, plunging. Caught in the crossfire of wind and water Osprey reaches, and cannot, and rises, and falls back, and only on the third and final try finds his wings. And he has what he came for. And he will race now for home. Circling wide between breakwater and land he shirrs the stinging salt from eyes and shoulders. Slung by Osprey's blooded talons a yellowjack rides toward the horror that awaits, alive, and immobile as Fate...

Night. The Protector of Fishes sits on the edge of his narrow berth and contemplates the boats he has known and the days spent there. He cannot remember the count and so cannot decide if they were too many or not enough. They were long days. That is all he knows. Countless the fishes dead by his hand and the winch he ran:

> Eight Bells, toes curled against the cold he feels the wheelhouse rove in a following sea; Eyes closed, even in deep sleep he sees the fishes gasping and flapping in the bluedark of the ice hold when they should have been long dead.

He closes the Book and speaks: "To say the Compassion of the Lord is Infinite is to say the Suffering of the World is without limit and did God make the one and not the other?"

The day is coming when The Protector of Fishes will eat no flesh and content himself with loaves and memories. After a point, all killing is the same.

WINTER

Monarch Migration

It is seven o'clock on Autumn's Eve and the Monarchs are in migration. One by one by one royal butterflies, cadmium yellow and burnt orange outlined in heavy Rouault black, come down the coastal corridor that is their roadway, rush hour in the sky. Some magnet we cannot feel draws them, south and south and south. Even though the prevailing winds remain against them. Even though weather is still warm; even though the dread of winter is a far and foreign form. They cannot help themselves. Cannot stay. Must go on.

They fly low. All you need do is look up to see them, opposite that deep unclouded blue. Straight as paper kites run onto the storm they dip, and rise, a fluttering stained glass transparency. They do not feed, or rest. On and on they fly though the goal they are seeking with such urgency, such single mind, will be their own death.

Migration of the Monarch Butterfly is no ordinary journey. Its days are butterfly years. They separate parent from offspring absolutely, requiring not one life but many to complete, a transit of thousands of miles and many generations like a journey to the stars. At each station Monarchs will mate, and lay their eggs, and die there. From each egg the caterpillar with his poled warning of white and black and yellow will emerge to feed upon the milkweed where it was born. Then from a blueprint known only to itself it will forge the jewel case of a chrysalis and within, grounded caterpillar will transform into a thing that flutters and soars. When at last the hinge snaps open a newborn butterfly emerges, unrecognizable. Does Caterpillar remember itself in this new-crowned elegance? Does Butterfly recall that first caterpillaring form? Monarch dries her wings to rise, and travel on.

Monarch migration has no instruction book and leaves no trace, neither pheromone nor formula. How does one age inherit from another such imperatives? Why did Evolution choose such a long highway? Perhaps continents once joined have drifted carrying the summering and wintering ranges with them, eons becoming miles, miles generations, the way mapped in the blood. Or perhaps the land stayed where it was and climate did not and the distance between warm and cold spread apart on its own. Perhaps both are true, and perhaps neither. Even Monarch does not know.

Once in your life you may discover an entire tree a-shimmering, Monarchs in the midst of their great journey home. Look for them on the east side, away from wind, that in the morning they will face the rising sun. There they will shiver themselves awake. And flex their wings. And one by one by one break free and carry on. Our hearts go with them and with the heart the mind together gathered and uplifted, into ... thin ... air ...

The View from Land's End

The sea comes crashing and smashing in to shore. You would not think so much violence would build in such a narrow space, Long Island Sound hardly a bath of water, twelve miles broad. But that is enough. A small boat in trouble here and no one would know it. You could die here, and never be found.

This is the same sea that was calm as a tucked sheet. The sun beat down from a sky with no clouds in it, the day warm and sleepy and at sunset, a bright gibbous moon, glistening.

Close your eyes.

Inhale.

Exhale.

Open your eyes and the water is torn to pieces. Waves break apart long before they beach, ripping the weed from its moorings, throwing stones. Even the crabs are drowned, lying limp-legged on their backs among the dull detritus of mussel shells littering the surf line, empty blue corpses. All this, and only a taste of what the sea can become.

Breakers are born from friction as water climbs that shallowing wedge of bottom speeding toward land. The long swell, almost imperceptible out on the deep becomes Leviathan inshore. And yet, though wind whips the surf, the swell beneath was not made here. The fury was already in it.

A narrow island, the fossil remnant of glaciers long gone is all that separates this little pond from the vast Atlantic. Out there it piles up unopposed. Out there, it does what it wants. It builds and builds sometimes to terrible proportions. The greatest liners, the biggest ships have seen their bows stove in and deck plates broke in two. So much for the Works of Men astride the Colossus of the Sea.

Never trust yourself to the mercies of the sea. We fear what lies beneath with reason. Unknown. Unknowable. There is no dominion there. Only ignorance resides in the sea and a power beyond our control or comprehension.

We know more about the center of our galaxy than the benthic folds and trenches, dark within dark in a wine dark ocean.

Nothing on earth is as humbling as the sea, the hungry, churling, gnarly Sea. It consumes our hubris in one swallow and though we do not like it, deep down, we know.

How Ducks Dive

Ducks come in two flavors, ducks that dive and ducks that don't. The "don't dive" ducks are Dabblers. You will find them working the shallows almost anywhere. Ballasted by feet and feathers, operated by competing demands of sustenance and the need for oxygen they bob and balance as they feed.

Tail up, head down.

Tail down, head up.

Diving Ducks are ducks of a different color (Fancy That) with very different ways. They fly underwater the way ordinary birds fly through air. Oh the panic of the little fishes with Diving Ducks in close pursuit, twisting turning spinning as the fishes do. But if you take for granted that Diving Ducks merely dive, you are mistaken. They leap!

The webbed feet of mergansers and buffleheads, of surf scoters, loons, and cormorants are spring-loaded levers, as taut as the sinewed limbs of Olympians. Those feet propel their owners clean out of water, momentarily suspended. Then, along the natural arch of that momentum head first down they go, plunging deep, and only a ripple to show where they have been.

Meanwhile the Dabblers dabble unperturbed. Like people living near a highway, or a skyway, when Diving Ducks come speed-diving through, Dabblers let them pass without notation or complaint. "No drama," the Dabblers would say.

Head up, tail down.

Head down, tail up.

Below, holding breath till lungs burn like a welder's arc the Diving Ducks race on, fire underwater. Do they glance as they turn sidewise from below at their cud-chewing cousins? Do they envy the Dabblers, metronome of the customary and the commonplace for their long inhale, cool exhale, and the leisure of their pace?

Diving Ducks, after they disappear, reappear again. The day may come when they don't but that is not up to them. As to the Dabblers coasting on the placid surface, if not the first to go they will surely be the first to see it coming.

It's Too Damn Hot

By calendar and by account it is the dreaded dead-dark of winter. Except that it is not. The air feels like Spring. The light looks like Spring. It smells like Spring, that moist effulgence green with melt and renewal when snow is impossible and life is about to break out, to explode. January never felt so bold and the guilty truth is something is amiss, but I like it. And how do you reconcile that?

I'm mulling this over on someone's waterfront porch drinking a steaming hot espresso, trespassing. The owners are in Florida or Antibes (or Terra del Fuego for all I know), wherever it is they go to escape the winter. They

might as well stayed home. It's sixty degrees, I should
have ordered that espresso on ice.

What I'm doing here (aside from enjoying the weather
and breaking the law) is taking pictures, after the same
flock of red-breasted mergansers I've been trying to pho-
tograph for months. They have this thing they do—Speed
Diving I call it—where they form a line and swimming
and diving and swimming and diving they drive the bait-
fish forward. A movable feast, and a slaughter. The time
to capture this is early when the day is cold and the sea
flat calm and the light is from the right direction, and
with the lens I have (which is half as long as it should be
for this kind of work), they need to be in close. Crouched
behind the bars of the porch rail, camera braced against
an upright and the shutter speed fast as an early morning
sun will allow, I'm ready. All they have to do is reappear.
Right there.

Twenty-four in imperfect artillery rows go under, a
timed barrage, one after the other. It is that cannonade of
a dive I want, the lift and push of cadmium orange feet,
bodies arched, leaving the water to torpedo into it again
then sounding deep and the eddy of their wake recoils
behind them. As fast beneath as they are above you must
be quick to predict where they pop up and quicker still to
catch it.

And of course I don't. Not the way I wanted.

Turning, they make another run still further out.
That's what they do, not only back and forth but at each

pass a greater distance from the shore. It will be afternoon before they tack, once more turning landward. But I am out of time, and out of patience too. I rise to go and as I do I realize the mergansers are not diving, they are dancing.

Drakes salute and bow to their would-be lovers who if they are impressed don't show it. Open-mouthed, anxious as teenage boys they call their high soft calls, scoot and scurry, dip and prance. But when one is accepted (more perhaps out of boredom than passion) the girl in question will lower her head as if her bill were filled with fangs and vanquish all except her intended. It might have looked like this when Odysseus waded in among the suitors except, for the mergansers, though swords are brandished no blood is drawn and it's Penelope who does the culling.

This is the ritual of courting, a full month earlier than I have ever seen it. What to make of this? I'd rather not. Easier to pretend the Dance never ends. Easy to enjoy the heat when cold is what is wanting. Easy to forget how we lay uneasy in our beds, tepid, tossing, throwing off the coverlets when the very next day the temperature drops and the whole thing stops as if it never started.

When you're hot, you're hot. And when you're not?

Bluebill, Broadbill, Blackhead, Scaup: Too Many Names, Not Enough Ducks

False horizon, scaup form a thin dark line upon the winter sea. Like toys, bobbing high, they let the current carry them, and the wind. Sometimes one bathes. Sometimes one stands like a child in a high chair and stretches, arms flapping. Though they are diving ducks what you will not see them do is dive. Too early in the day, these are only preparations.

Females, except for that milky daub at the base of the bill are dark all over. The males from this distance appear

black on head and tail and have bodies of ivory. It's easy
to tell the one from the other. What is nearly impossible
at more than a few yards is to tell Greater scaup from
Lesser. It matters. Habit and habitat are diverse between
the two, and who knew the numbers would fall the way
they've done? If you want to know the count, ask a man
who guns.

The Grouper is my source for all things Duck. In season, every chance he can, he's out there. It's a Marine Corp
thing except the ducks don't shoot back. Only the weather
does that.

"Sleet? Never heard of it. Storm warning? What kind
of a sissy do you think I am?"

The Grouper is your man if you want to know what is
and what is not.

Lately, the answer is *"Not."*

"How'd you do?"

Greater scaup was what The Grouper bagged, but he
did not know about the flock. "Too far away," he said. "I
only know when I have one in my hands."

Greater scaup winter principally on our saltwater
coasts, all the way down into Mexico. Lesser scaup prefer
ponds and inland wetlands but this will not help you
because they also cleave to the waters just offshore. It
is possible to tell them apart by the males, lesser's head
having a purplish sheen and greater reflecting green, but
to see that, the light must be perfect. From shore I have
made the distinction only once. And if you cannot tell

lesser from greater it is very hard to tell how each one is doing except we already know the larger bird is in rapid decline and in all probability the small is not far behind.

The coastal habitat of our waterfowl used to be the greatest wetlands in the world—the Fens, the Meadow-lands, and all the major salt marshes in every cove between—just where we've built our great cities back to the days of the Pioneers and like them, water for us whether tidal or stream-fed is a toilet and a rubbish bin. These once-rich wintering and breeding grounds have largely been filled in or poisoned by a toxic brew.

"We only see seven or eight flocks of scaup a year now," The Grouper laments. I know what he means. There were *thousands* . . .

The weather came up hard, sleet, snow, sheet ice. I-95's a Demolition Derby, no time to be out and was I ever glad to get off the road. And wouldn't you know, just as I pull into the driveway it's The Grouper driving past, heading home with the duck boat in tow. He rolled the window down and told me the reason was not the storm. "Left the key on," he said, "battery's dead." Otherwise he'd be out there now, into all the terrors open ocean has to offer because he knows, the day will come (and he may live to see it) when all there is to do is sit, the Rem-ington idle across your lap remembering, how it used to be, and will not be, under a leaden sky bereft of wings.

Anatidae Dialectics

At the bend in the river a flock of mallards is dozing in tallgrass that is winter-bleached and battered by snow, by wind, by high water. Worn thin, there is little cover in it but it is all the mallards have and must make do. In these river narrows, in the tie-down of the straights and shallows their only true refuge is daysleep. The pulse drops, the body stops except for the low breath and the least heat it needs to keep on living. Even the sun is cold. And the mallards hold.

They are an average flock, these mallards. Still as the ice grounded to the bank. Closest are four drakes, laid up with their bills tucked to the crook at the back of their necks. Positioned this way their heads are a virtual black so dark it is not a color but a gap. Sensing my presence the drakes, in consort, look up. And a curious thing. That gap fills with an iridescence, so brilliant, reminiscent more of a scarab's shell than the soft hue of feathers.

It is the angle between the shafts. Heads bent, the feathers spread. Light falls straight in and vanishes. Only when the drakes unfurl themselves do the feathers relax and close and the full green flash of plumage, bright as a lighthouse, beacons forth.

The object of all this stands between them, a single hen, invisible as an afterthought. Movement reveals her and (now that she is standing) so do her very orange feet. The color is a sign that breeding is imminent, though the choosing is not yet complete. It is for her the drakes risk themselves this way and hide as best they can when they sleep. For the need runs deep and the mallards stay.

I want to lie down beside them there on the spongy bank, nestle my face into the warm hollows of their wings and feel the pulse and listen to them breathe. But I must leave. Not out of fear nor because I am riven by the frigid air and not because I want to. I am comforted here. As if I belong here. As I am sure we used to before we knew what we know and wish we did not.

Chimera

Inscribed in mud. No scribe made them. Cuneiform of journeys inadvertently revealed. Artifact of intentions not intended to be seen.: Muskrat came this way. See her paws spelled out and those of her progeny. Next, Raccoon. Wakened by the too-warm-weather and taking his groggy time as if in a fever dream. White-footed mouse, hurry hurry hide hide. Tracks emerging. Tracks collide. Into the salt marsh tracks return. Among the hummocks and the dry stumps of the sedges, between the brittle stalks of spartina, each entrance, every exit is recorded.

Save for one.

Scrawled left and right like rough quotation marks,

these are the words they set apart: "Life." It arrives from no place. "Death." It vanishes into no where. The pen is the sharp of talon. The ink, red of blood. Underlined by a hard unlettered sign, the abstract signature of beak wiping itself clean: Harrier! A whisper in the scream.

Face of Owl, Eye of Hawk, Span of Golden Eagle ending in feather-fingered wings. The hooked nose of Falcon. The claws of a Griffin. How gently he sweeps and tips and turns. How close and easy he comes, barely topping the salt grass and only at the last one quick snap and away.

Here the Chimera of Herakles. Beware!

There is a relationship between the size of the thing observed and its apparent speed. Preternaturally large always seems interminably slow, until it is upon you. Sight Northern Harrier in flight and see for yourself. Bigger than he appears he is faster than he appears. The simplicity, the great economy, barely a wing beat and how the cedars blur with the speed of his traverse, single-minded as the arrow as it leaves the bow. His gaze, straight down, is unwavering. No movement escapes him. Even the periphery of vision serves him and what visions he can see. Traces left by mouse are bright as yellow carnotite glowing under black light. Tracks, black intaglio on brown are Technicolored. Ultraviolet, infrared, dusk, day, all illuminate that hawkish eye, incite that avian brain. Nor is the owl-like cupping of the sockets without design for these focus sound. Burrow, nest, the well-trod path beneath the reeds matted and rafted in the tidal rush are no re-doubt for rabbit or jumping mouse or vole. Sparrow sings at his peril. Mole squeals at her risk. Not one note missed.

Hovering, Harrier glides in and circles round then falls. Feet scuff and scrimble in erasure on that spongy ground. Beak descends. Levers side to side till head jerks back. Too far away to hear the tendons snap.

Time passes. Harrier lifts, and drifts, and turns one last time, white undermarkings of body and wings the semaphore of his good-bye. Where he has been, I don't go there. I have no need to turn that page. There are words understood without being seen. There are texts that are known without being read.

Adopt-a-Gull

T is the season when the outdoors moves in. Mice, content to scutter through the wild grasses of summer and the leaf mulch of early fall, upon the Winter Solstice come calling. They secret through the crevices in walls and into drawers and cupboards, and make a larder there. How many times have I found a mouse nest (ball of hay and seed and bits of wool) in among the garden gloves in the storage bin, or between the old towels saved for spring cleaning? Spiders, backed into retreat, find the warm corners of ceilings or cellars there to enjoy the winter darkness. Even the ladybugs come indoors, waking improvidently to an occasional false and lethal than, unreliable as thin ice, which will draw them from their hiding places in the first or second month of the year. Of course, not all of them will be fooled. When Winter melts away the survivors will return to the rosebushes as they have done, always.

The animals that do not come inside also make use of our homes. There is a young opossum, a commuter, who sleeps in the crawlspace several days a week. In the garage a stray cat sometimes sojourns. Gone as wild as the things she hunts it's as close to home as she knows. I've found the tracks of a family of raccoons below the deck and once, a rounding in the gravel under the truck where the engine made it warm, was that night's raccoon bedroom. Having replaced what had always been *Theirs* with *Ours,* those that survive adapt to us, as if we are only the latest iteration of the landscape. They take advantage when and where they can.

The gull who sits on the chimney cap soaking in those rising calories of combustion does not need to do this. All through the hardest season you will find him astride the waves in weather so dire the spray freezes on the rocks. But for now the time is opportune and the chimney is a free fare, and no one to prevent him from enjoying it. He will fly away. The mouse will move out. The cat might find a real home for herself if she has that kind of luck and chooses to take it.

Our situation, unlike the animals, is neither flexible nor fortunate. Miss a mortgage payment and see where that will take you. Lose your job and it could be you living on a heating grate. Unlike the gull, guaranteed someone will shoo you away. Come a day it may be you and me who comes a-calling, and the *mouse* who will not let *us* in. Next time you set a trap, think of that.

The Darkest Season
of the Year

The salt grass, gone from blue-green to tawny yellow has at last turned to tarnished silver in the blushing cold. That blush belongs to us alone, all color having left this place a while ago, all except for the ruddy weathers in our winded faces. What remains, earthen tones of decay in all their tone-deaf stages, this bleached result, will endure longer than it seems we can endure. A sidereal dark extending behind us and before us.

The marshland sways, silent even in the wind. A dense and dour nothingness in which the unassuming eye sees nothing, the Gray of Nature, a coverlet thick as an eiderdown, one that captures cold not heat. But wait. There! In the high spartina—Is that a throat an ear a beak?

Stare.

Rub your lids.

Freeze in your tracks.

Where you look, someone looks back.

Spy-hopping, an American Bittern peeps not up but out, beak and neck and body in line with the trace the Sou'Wester makes as it rakes the grass to a scudding angle. That angle is his camouflage. The stripes he wears are nuanced to the shades and shadows of the marsh in wind and except for luck, invisible to the likes of me. Though I have him in the crosshairs he appears and disappears as he will.

Inland, just out of sight of Bittern's salt domain a brackish channel lies. The Saracen edge of the Solstice slaughtered the sedges and sabercut the leafy flesh of the bayberry to the bone. Storm-sheared, *Rosa rugosa,* once ripe with color is all a crackling mass of thorns. Self-pruned branches of pine and oak litter the tidemark, bolstered there by sheaves of broken reeds. They lie high and dry until they blanch or the fungi and the lichens grind them finely into dust. Out here over time the biggest anchor turns to rust.

But look: One branch one stalk one stump or stubborn vine inclines itself too much to the vertical to be true in the midst of all this tangle and destruction. Only this and the unblinking glint of pupil black as deep of space gives Great Blue Heron away. I have often wondered how those streaks and spots and nuanced grays work for her, so large, nothing could function as a hide. Across this vast and small divide we stand straight up and down and eye-to-eye.

There are two seasons only. In one, Nature is reborn, a time of wakefulness, of restoration. The other is a time of rest. Of gathering in. We sometimes call it Winter, and it is here. Hold close. Be of good cheer. The life that lights this place is always near.

Have Yourself a Merry Little Christmas

I have always been a sucker for Christmas lights. Not, you understand, those elegant whites like illuminated flakes of ice. I am talking color, gaudy as a traffic signal, blazing primaries that do not even blink. Alone in the backseat driving to my grandfather's house at dusk, escaping the dark humors of the place where I grew up I would look into the windows of the slums next door to the slum where we lived, not thinking of that, but of how welcoming those places were with all the lamps burning bright and the shades still open wide. At our apartment we lived in a perpetual blackout. The Great Depression was far enough away it was meaningless to me but for my parents the heat went down at night and the light bulbs lasted about forever. Even the front entrance was in darkness. As if there was no one home.

At Grampa and Gramma's it was not like that. My grandfather had been a cigar roller in Haymarket Square. Until a few years ago the faded sign was still visible on the building: Hand Rolled Cigars. It was barely a living. Then in 1921 his friend Jake Green came and told him Prudential was hiring. My grandfather was dead forty years before I realized this was code for *hiring Jews*. Like the banks, insurance companies did not do that. But he stood in line and got lucky and they took him on. It was pure self-interest. They needed people who could sell policies to Polish and Russian and Yiddish speakers and he was fluent in all those languages and English and a little Italian I think, and did well, and in Chelsea (where analogous to "hiring" they were now "selling") he bought a two-decker with a yard and in the thirties a car, which was unheard of. In that house the lights were always blazing when we arrived, but even there they went out when we left, and I remember him walking three long flights down to the coal cellar to fire up the hot water heater for when it was needed, and again to turn it off.

I never questioned that cold and frugal night into which I had been born but light meant a lot as early as I can remember. The strings of bulbs and wires the firemen strung. Chanukah candles. Those yellow-warm windows and the imagined welcoming inside, to which I was denied.

The woods are leafless now, dark as any distant habitation where all light comes from open starlit sky. The marsh and its surroundings have solidified to earthen browns and shale grays as pale as silt. And the day is short. And all the birds of Fall are flown. On a far-off steeple grackles roost, decorations upon the cutout simulacrum of an evergreen, awaiting there the miserly warmth of a rising winter sun. At the edge of the salt pond a single winterberry stands, its berries electric red, as bright as any man-made ornament. They are edible those berries, but the birds have not come to eat. We flock to the colors, them and me. Downy Woodpecker with his punk hair. Northern Mockingbird, that canary diamond-of-an-eye all asparkle. Bluejay in his best blue suit and Warbler in her off-season coat, the one with only a hint of yellow feather. I make no attempt to hide. Standing in plain sight I look at them, they look at me. We share this, Illuminated Symmetry.

Avian Algebra

Early this morning I spotted a bird of prey on a weathered pine pole. She'd made a kill and sat there digging in, chunking down the red raw meat. Between each rip and tear were quick glances right, left, and occasionally at me. It was too late to determine what kind of creature she was eating except it once had feathers. She herself was determinate. The identifying alphanumeric was an inverted L-shaped stripe at her brow, the original Horus Eye, dark and stark and personal as a nameplate. Bigger than Kestrel (+K), smaller than Peregrine (−P), it's not every day you see one, and almost never as close to hand: Falcon + K − P = *Merlin*. Q.E.D.

After the kill is devoured Merlin will stop to clean (Cn) and preen (Rn). Dirty ragged feathers are neither elegant nor efficient, and speed, accurate trajectory, maneuverability must be invariant in the Math of Merlins. Downtime between hunts while tempered by grooming must also factor Volume Eaten (Ve) divided by rate of Digestion (D), which translates to a polynomial: $(Cn + Rn) \times (Ve \div D) = Ravenous$. The answer to "Am I hungry?" is therefore always "Yes!"

If Hunger is a Constant, "Are you Edible?" is its operand which in turn is a function of size. Merlin's basic food group is the Tasty Little Bird (TLB) and she will take both land and shore species and in season dragonflies, all of the above mostly on the wing. Although she consumes (when she can get it) one-third her body weight each and every day, there is a limit to the mass of any individual kill. Which is to say, bigger than a beetle, smaller than a chipmunk or in the particular case of Me:

$$MSL \div TLB = WAY\ TOO\ BIG\ (WTB)$$

Since Merlin is still eating and I am not a candidate for immediate disembowelment, only one variable remains undefined, namely, "Are you too close?" Consider the Cat. Cats, big and small, always merit caution. But how much? And at what range? That hunkering down, the casual or careful pad of terrible and silent feet—body language is the modulus of danger when it comes to Cats. Likewise for Owl, whose warning posture is no more than a silent stare must be gauged for risk and avoided, or evaded. Owl extends no professional courtesies and will catch Merlin if he can, dividing her into parts as she divides what she eats. Therefore, threat is not by species nor distance nor intent but an algorithm of all three, an Imaginary Number only Merlin knows which yields the answer: Stay or Flee.

Who would suspect Merlin's soft and gentle face harbors a brain of such cold-blooded calculus? What Avian Algebra will keep Merlin safe in such concise proximity to Human being, here among these meager vanishing weeds?

White Noise

When Eskimo talk of snow, their words are whole sentences, based on look and texture and if the crystals are small or big and how they fall and gather, or do not, and whether it will stay or go away, and what it is good for and also how it sounds. We, poor relations, who think six inches is snow when northern peoples barely shrug at anything less than six feet, we have one word only. All by itself. Don't let this fool you. Don't be misled by some tobogganing of the mind down that slippery slope of inattention. Our snow does fine.

There is Snow that falls discretely in tiny grainy knots when it is almost too cold to snow, as dry as a product of water can be dry and still be water: *Snow*, said-all-at-once.

There is that half-inch of ash coating the path that barely provokes a yawn, Sa, ah, ahhh, noooo . . .

And the four-inch slush when the car won't go without a tow, Szr! Szr! Sza-sza-sza-sza-sza, Znow.

The snow that has formed and thawed and frozen again and bites your cheeks till they are red, and rages in the wind sibilant and hard as sand is Tssssssssssssno, tsssss . . .

The stuff of flakes flat and sparkling like mica in a cement sidewalk, that crinkles where you step and goes, ch-Snow! ch-Snow! ch-Snow!

There is a snow that is wet and comes in clumps and lands in bumps on hats and gloves, SSSDOH.

And the one so lithe it blows like smoke while it whispers that word in white, PSSSSSSnowwww.

There is the Snow that melts as it lands like a fish out of water (throw that one back), and the

Snow ❄

that grows ❄

to the size of ❄ (this big) in a child's imagination when she has a cold hardly worth a tissue and a blow, and you won't let her go out! Snow, woe, woe ****

Wind is the Voice of Snow and when it stops there is

only Silence. In the morning when it has snowed all night people cozy to the fire (if they have one), around corn-cakes or apple fritters on the old stove (if they don't) and they eat, and are full, and sit and watch the Snow. Some day, Commerce with the aid of Science will eliminate Winter altogether and with it, the Solitude of Silent Con-templation and the last best thing that holds Civilization at bay, and makes us Human.

Esau's Portion

My grandmother's whole family died of diabetes. Mother, father, six brothers and sisters. They went blind. They lost feet. They lost limbs. One voice, then another became silent and as to the others in the country left behind, "Hitler," my grandmother used to say, "took care of them." She was a Polish Jew; that part of the story is not unique but it made the remnant smaller and except for me, she died alone.

Both of my grandparents sang to me. I remember sitting in my grandfather's lap, comforted by his wordless quasi-liturgical crooning, the rocking chair rolling, a ship at safe harbor. My grandmother's singing was different, songs with words, sung mostly at the enamel-topped kitchen table and always while I was eating, the sun pouring in. Of the two of them it was my grandmother who was religious, but what she sang about was birds. "Four little chickadees sitting in a tree, one flew away and then there were three..." Our family's love of birds descends from her. Our politics came from the men though they too fed the birds. Birds became Wildlife, Wildlife became Nature, Nature became Synthesis.

When I wake in the morning what I do first thing is make sure the feeders are full, and for those who prefer not to stand in line I spread a scoop of seed on the deck rail. Part of it stays, part of it falls to the deck, the rest to the ground. Everyone is accommodated. This, before I make breakfast or even coffee. That part is biblical: If the animals are hungry you must feed them before you feed yourself. The wobbly waking raccoon who appears by the light of half a moon on the odd warm winter night, even she finds something to eat. No one leaves here hungry. That part is political: From Each to Each (Means, to Need). That means are limited and need is not is a modern fact of life.

Now all in all there are too many mouths, and righteous intention cannot change it. I say this not out of parsimony or revision, but out of worry. Every day there is less room. Fewer trees. Less openness. The bulldozer skirts as close to the salt marsh as the law allows, and then, that much closer. The commonplace becomes rare, the uncommon fleeting, something you will likely miss and never see again. The well-manicured lawn becomes our epitaph.

"Look, a white bird!" Valerie says and I turn just in time to see the tail end of it but enough of a glimpse to be certain this was something out of the ordinary. I toss the lenscap, brace the camera against the windowsill and we wait, knowing, most times you only get the one chance and we'd had that already. But the bird comes back and for the five biggest minutes of the day we watch him fly from thistle feeder to phragmites to feeder and finally, into the cedars and gone. Where he came from, if there are more or many or only him, who can say? We have not seen him since, and we won't.

If you take the train, any train, passenger or boxcar from city to suburb to country you will be moving from Present into Past. Go the other way and as the houses crowd together, the highways gather lanes and speed, the trees become thinned then absent altogether you will be traveling from your present into a future that, if you think about it, you do not want. Not for yourself. Not for anyone. And if you don't have the price of a ticket you can sit where you are, perfectly still, and see the land cut away one leg at a time, one voice after another snuffed out. Progress itself is our undoing. Chainsaw is our swansong, all the lessons come after the fact and perhaps the only antidote is just—Stop.

Birds on Ice

The herring gulls are standing on the pond. Not swim-ming, standing. They skid and slide, old ladies trying to cross from trolley to sidewalk and not a Boy Scout in sight. Old lady falls? Void the warrantee. Gulls? Fact of the matter is they don't fall or if they ever do don't seem much worried about it. Won't break a hip, those gulls, a wrist a leg a rib which does not explain why they are here instead of somewhere at the least out of the wind!

Why are they doing this?

Gull falls through. The water hovers at 32 and you'd be dead in eight minutes. Nightmare scenario—for you. For the gull? It's an opportunity for a bath, leisurely and refreshing. Gull hops out, slip and slide and don't even reach for a towel, then skid clumsy as a—duck out of water? Utterly ridiculous.

Why are they doing this?

Heat loss in water is much more rapid than in air. In air molecules are orders of magnitude farther apart than in water. This means an object in air has fewer collisions with those molecules. Each collision transfers energy— Heat. Fewer collisions, less heat loss. This is why when it's cold, windchill is so important. The greater the wind-speed, the larger the absolute number of molecules col-liding with a living body and the faster that body transfers heat—and freezes. Therefore, except in a high wind, gulls fare better out of water, even when the only out is on ice.

On a morning like this when the thermometer reads barely 20 degrees I'm not sure where the point of equi-librium lies, where moving air steals more heat than still water. Except if it were only a matter of that, gulls would never get their feet wet. In winter, salt water unlike fresh is only 28 degrees but you will find the gulls out there day and night and doing fine. On a morning like this with a surface slush of sea ice you'd be dead in . . . three minutes.

In their tolerance the gulls are not alone. All the water-birds are unperturbed by cold water. The ability to segre-gate the circulation in their feet, the best insulation system Nature ever made, a high metabolism, all conspire to serve them. In the face of such perfection, hard to argue ice serves solely as a refuge from cold water. Mallards gravitate to ice and gamble there, geese climb on board in the river at night, cormorants land on ice and think nothing of it, skidding to a halt somewhere down the line. Perhaps they feel more safe on solid water, thick enough to support them, thin enough no coyote can venture near without falling through. Or it might be habit, a pond or watercourse they are used to, where they usually go, whose change in elemental state from their point of view is neither salutary nor reprobate.

All these may be true but I think the attraction of waterbirds to ice is the same as a child to puddles. One, always forced to be dry, can't resist getting her feet wet. The other, always wet, marvels at the novelty of stepping in with feet still dry.

Ducks Boarding Surf

The sea is cast in metallic winter light. It glints like the polish of Turkish canon, waiting. Near at the water's edge the rounded stones are capped with ice, the knitted kepis of sun-bleached men, dug in, afraid to go and rightly so. Only the winter ducks dare enter this cold desert of water. Red-breasted Mergansers with mohawk crests, thick-throated Loons, the soft-eyed Mallards, marshmallow-topped Buffleheads. You can see them all from here but not today. Today, Black Duck rules.

The Black Duck is mostly brown and on each wing a slash of violet. Their given name makes sense only against a bright white sky or at a late hour. It is that hour now.

Having dallied dabbling here at the rocky line of the tide, like small dark boats, through the turbulent surf Black Ducks must go, out to the paradoxical shelter of open water. The muttering wave towers over. It freezes in the foam. They sally back and forth timing their run, infantry timing a charge to the booming and the silence of the guns. The flock steadies. Readies. The sea breaks. Black Ducks crane their necks to look across the battle smoke of water. It breaks again and into the smashing surf and through the breach they go!

The water under them below the dire swells is colder than ice. The air above is colder still. How do they endure? Why don't they fly, away, south, west, anywhere but here? But their feathers do not damp, do not collapse against the skin or drag them under as our mock down coats would do. Even so, though they have charged beneath the canon and past the stinging shrapnel of the spray, paddled out beyond where waves hold sway, still they are at war.

Black Ducks are in steep decline, no one knows exactly why. One day only the story will survive, of their pluck and valor. This was a sight I may not see next year. Well on their way, not a one looks back.

Greater Scaup in Lesser Light

L ate in the day when the light is puddle-shallow and even the deeps feel thin and narrow, the ducks gather in. It is only frigid cold that sends them here. For, when the marsh freezes and the rivers are solid as a white brick road this is their last and only liquid place to roost, on the waves of the winter ocean.

Wary, ready to touch and go they will come sweeping low, the Belt of Venus all aglow behind them. See them now, beating to wind'ard in a long wide turn as they survey the sea below. Searching . . . seeking . . . for others of their kind which conveys safety, and for us who are by nature a danger. Because of this if you want to find them you must stay as hidden as you can, in dark clothing, not moving, keeping watch leeward of the rocks and patient as a stone.

First a flock of mallards comes, all drakes in green and violet tartan. Oak-leafing in, dumping the air from their wings they line up for landing until they see me and flee scattershot. Moments later a red-breasted merganser makes his flyby, webbed feet spanking water to a spray as he too realizes his mistake, then off fast-flying in a blur. A pair of black ducks do not come close at all, calling their disapproval as they vanish into the twilight, angry voices fading.

Wind blows. Hands hurt. Patience thins. Just as I am ready to give in a flight of greater scaup appears. Rising, they pass straight over, the last ruddy flare of the sun painting their bodies with light. They turn away and at first I think I've lost them also but it is only part of their pattern and they turn again, laying in straight toward me.

Reaching for ground effect speed drops, wings propped with air, bellies barely above the waves. I would like to think they recognize my harmlessness. It is unlikely. Either I am undiscovered in this last frigid light or they've chosen to ignore me, too cold too tired now to leave. They shake themselves as they settle, and it amazes me as it always does that the salt sea is their comfort and their harbor. How much more than me they must need this lee we share . . .

Quietly, I slip away.

Sunrise. An oily coat of sea ice hovers inshore flattening the water to a strange and artificial calm. Just beyond, it is rough as a file. The mergansers and mallards, black ducks and scaup of the day before are nowhere to be seen and I wonder how many have not survived the night.

Animal Personals

Desperately seeking Foxy Lady. SM Red Fox, 59, nice coat, seeks sleek female of the species 29 to 38. I'm barking mad for ya, baby. Not mechanically inclined (No Kits).

My clock is ticking. Lonely SF Gray Fox, 39, full-figured gal with own burrow and established territory searching for the right canid for LTR and the whole Kit and caboodle.

DF Mourning Dove, 42, Pleasing shape, good nest builder, tired of the single life and ready to settle down seeks M 40–60 for LTR.

DM Mourning Dove, 45, looking for the Racing Pigeon of my dreams. Must be sleek, fast flier, 18 to 28

light-phase preferred, must like to travel. No nest build-
ers please!

Croon in June, under the full Moon we'll Swoon. SM
Coyote 63, never married, seeks F 20–24. Great markings a must.

SF Coyote, 58, Plain Jane with a Technicolor heart
seeks the man of her dreams, for duets, sunsets, and possible Long-term Howl?

Had a bellyful? Want a change of diet? Can't carrion
alone? No more waiting for Natural Causes. Catch a ther-
mal with this hot DF Vulture. Let's get together and KILL
something!

She got the nest. But this DM Vulture, 51, nearsighted
and frankly not the best-looking guy in the sky, is still
hoping for someone who knows hair isn't everything.
Any SF Bald Eagles out there? Must be H/W/P 24–29.

SM Laughing Gull, great SOH, own slot at the dump.
What more could a bird be looking for? Peck my red spot
and I'll peck yours.

SF Laughing Gull, serious professional, done with being in the dumps, sick of "red-spot" jokes. Isn't there a
Bonaparte or even a Skua out there, anywhere?

Bye-Bye, Blackbird. Soon to be DM Crow, mature but
young at heart, seeks a raven-feathered beauty 17 to 39.
Let's do something to crow about. Pictures a must.

My soon to be Ex thought he was something to Crow
about. Not. This Raven, 48, a former Miss Yellowstone
who still has her sheen, seeking DM Raven 29–32 who's

made mistakes and wants to nestle under a guiding wing. I know where all the campers stop, we'll spread clean underwear all over the Park! (OK I admit it, shiny objects still get my attention ...)

I'm a thief and I dig it! Recently WW M Raccoon 29, pleasingly plump, knows every garbage can in town and willing to share, wants woman same age who knows how to stay out of traffic. I'll grow on ya. LTR definitely.

Racy WW F Raccoon 29 going on 18. I wanna cross the street for a guy who's nimble on his feet, ready for a getaway, and not afraid of traffic. Forget garbage. Let's rob a bank!

Dance to a different drummer. SM Downy Woodpecker, 37, successful professional with a major stash of acorns for a woman with rhythm! Must be H/W/P 21–25. I'm free as a bird and it fits my bill just fine.

30-ish F Downy Woodpecker, tired of hollowing out her own tree, looking for Papa, and baby makes three? I'm eggs-actly what you're looking for. LTR only!

MM M Skunk 42 but looks a lot younger, pleasingly *gras*, seeks *petit fois* for *ménage à trios* and possibly more, but skunks can only count to four.

MM F Skunk filing for divorce. Does anyone know a good lawyer?

My hubby isn't having any and all I wanna do is to Paint the Town Red. Flit on over for a weekend of fun with this MM F Cardinal. Discretion a must—but not to worry, he's on a religious retreat.

MM GM Cardinal seeks same. Must LOVE Cole Porter: "Birds do it!" Discretion a must. These secular females can make your life Hell, but not to worry, she thinks I'm on a religious retreat. No fatties please.

Are you a Hot City Kitty or a green-eyed monster? If the former, this buff, tuff Puma's all male and on the prowl. Join in for fun forays to Central Park. That place is crawlin' with sweatpants! No commitments—Let's just go run someone down together. Lookout world, that $200 pair of New Balance ain't gonna help you now!

No more nights slinking around town for this Seriously Cool WW F Puma. Well-fed but still feline feline is looking for that one purrrfect fella who's ready to curl up in one comfortable place. Long naps in the sun... Fresh country air... Got Game? You bet. Catch you tomcatting around I'll scratch your eyes out (How do you think I got to be a widow?).

SM Redtail, a Prince among Hawks, wants to meet delightful voluptuous full-breasted SF Peregrine Falcon for fun, fast times, and the thrill of the kill. Your stoop or mine? LTR? NOT!

Mature Full-feathered SF Red-tailed Hawk keeping an eye out for a raptor with Vision, and NO pretensions. Whole family of Diving Ducks in the larder—what can you bring to the nest? LTR ONLY.

WW M Crested Merganser just emerging from a deep personal tragedy due to a hunting accident, seeks Diver who knows how to Duck. Let's start with a quick get-away. Long-term migration possible.

SF Mute Swan—Oh, come slip with me the surly bonds of earth, high in that sunlit silence what need of words, with you, my One-and-Only? I Love for Life. Make your nest mine, Valentine.

SM Mute Swan—But soft! What light through yonder open breaks and beckons. I will sail at your side till the Sun fails and the World stands still, and even after. I also love for Life! Dear Valentine, my nest is yours.

D—Divorced, G—Gay, MM—Married, S—Single, WW—Widowed, M—Male, F—Female

H/W/P—Height and Weight Proportionate, LTR—Long-term relationship, SOH—Sense of Humor

Bob-Bob-Bobbin' Along, Along

Robins have arrived in the snow. Not the kind of snow you can peck through or scratch away. Snow like a salt glaze, bluish white, pebbly and shiny and slick as glass. They skip and skid upon the unexpected hardness of early Spring. This is what the robins have arrived to.

There are at least a hundred. They blanket the yard like the snow they prance upon, snow that fell here on the coast only in inches, followed by hours of fine freezing hail. Where will they hide? In bushes without leaves? In trees with bare branches? What will they eat, these tuggers of worms, when all the worms in the world are fast asleep? Even if the tiny treading footsteps of the birds awakened them, could soft-bodied annelids, pushing and prodding and innocuous, crack that locked earthen door much less the icy hasp?

Between my yard and the next is a row of feral privet bushes. Feral because if they've ever been trimmed it was not by me. True confession? I hate privet. Hate the way it smells, the way it looks. What possible good could those ugly blue-black berries do if at the end of a long hard winter they are still there, dangling, a basket of stone fruit ignored by every hungry mouth to come this way all these starving months and days.

Except, that is exactly what the Robins are doing here. They are eating the inedible.

It is not as if it doesn't affect them. They stand dumbfounded on the snow, feathers bulging against cold and the apparent discomfort of what they have just consumed. It passes through them quickly or simply refuses to stay down. Purple stains spread against the whiteness. Yet, perched in the bushes or hopping between to find what has fallen they eat until there is nothing left, not a single berry. And the next time I look the Robins have gone.

It is as if they have vanished. They are not on the road. Not in the woods. None fly. Walking the edge of the salt marsh I pause and think perhaps like rats gorged on ratbane they have been driven to the river in desperate thirst and drowned there. But it is not illness. Only

the hour has carried them away, that universal hour, that
vacancy just before sleep.

   The marsh is silent as a pillow. Inhaling, the air still
tastes like winter but Robins show, You Don't Need a
Weatherman to Know Which Way the Wind Blows.

Mud Season

Snow lingered too long. Dirt settled on top of it. Oil. Axle grease. Cigarette butts, one filtered one not. Light bulb (broken). Three pennies, useless tokens. A used napkin. An orange skin. An empty flask of Bombay gin. Enjoyed for an instant, reviled for the duration, from pristine to filthy as sin, such is the fate of Snow.

Last night rain came and washed away all trace of used-up Snow. Can't say I miss it. Except, now we have Mud. Earth plus Water plus all-the-stuff-that-was-in-the-snow-and-on-it equals Mud and unlike snow, Mud cannot be washed away. All you can do is pray the wet part of Mud will evaporate which it doesn't, or drain which it would if it only had a place to go. The ground, *semifreddo* just below, is the Unindicted Co-Conspirator of Mud and every night when you're least on your guard and hoping tomorrow will surely bring Liberation, the substrate freezes anew trapping water in preparation for ... more ... Mud.

Early morning Mud (stealthy devil) always looks dry when in fact it is barely congealed. To further torment, fossilized at the parking spot is the perfect impression of your good shoes where they sank into the Mud. Next to that, the tiny divot where you dropped the car keys and the great greasy puddle into which the grocery bag fell when you bent to fish the car keys out. You would linger and gnash your teeth but you're already late for work, the sun is up and warm and you know what that's going to mean because—you still have to walk the dog.

The cat (who if not smarter, is a hell of a lot more practical) refuses to go out. The dog can't wait. "C'mon!" says the dog, "We're gonna miss it! Naw, forget that stupid leash, are you kidding me? You don't need a leash, you won't get lost, come on! We're gonna miss the Mud!"

The dog when it comes to Mud, is a living proximity fuse. He wants to embrace, to be One, most of all to run— through the Mud—as close to your just-pressed suit as possible. Then, but only after he laps up that thin gray layer of indeterminate origin like he thinks it's Champagne, he offers you his great, dripping, paw. You have to take it. You've been training him to give you his paw for months and after you do (your hand up to the cuffs now indistinguishable from that sopping canine limb) he decides it's time for the other tricks you've been working on. These are Speak, Sit, and Roll Over, after which (de rigueur) he shakes himself dry. All over you.

Framed between the bare limbs of the black cherry tree and nowhere near the Mud, the resident Redtail watches the Noh drama of your pantomime, the brushing scrapping dusting and decrusting, the shaking of head, the rolling of eye, and by these very signs divines the season. He hurries to pass it on to the Cooper's hawk, who tells the Sharp-shin, who shares the news with a clarion Crow who raises wing to mouth like a cupped hand and lets the whole world know:

Spring Thaw! Thaw! Thaw! Thaw!

Exit Strategy

If this be the Lamb, God help the Lion.

Bend the cedars one more bar and they will break and the shakes that used to be the roof go flying. The edges of the eaves are lifting, the walls pressing in like a bellows on every blow. The great black-backed gulls who brave this ragged air tear by on swept-back wings while the little birds come rocketing, too fast to tell their shapes much less their names. The weather more than threatening is voracious. And we are what it eats.

Yesterday the first osprey appeared, down the long run of the river. Across the near shore and over the hump of the grassy dune he hovered there to inspect the old nest he will once again make his own. And last night, with only stars for candlelight I saw the first raccoon, bleary-eyed and slow and still in thrall to the warmth of winter sleep. Both regret their lone arrivals now.

And how the Lion roars!

The cloud cracks, a line sharp as a crease in wet concrete across its back. The weather front is blue beneath and gray as ashes over. Like a dark pyroclastic flow it rolls and gathers, then passes above our heads, beating to destinations unknown. It leaves us lucky, blustery but high and dry. Elsewhere raindrops the size of quarters will be smashing the early crocuses to pulp, the snowdrops into slush. Feathers will find themselves so wet their colors run, and sodden fur will be pungent as smoke, and shivering.

After all it is the Season, and needs no other reason for these moods, this migraine hammering only the rocks don't mind. As for the lives that live in and about these marshes what else can they expect? There is nothing permanent in any Natural weather; they bide their time and wait it out. Finally morning comes, calm as a Buddha, his enigmatic smile no surprise.

Thus the Lion bids good-bye.

Great Blue Heron Leaping

Great Blue Heron wears the bleached marsh grasses like a beard. He has made himself small, just there, across the brackish shallow. Stilting at the water's edge a perfect liquid mirror captures him, reflection joined to the vanishing point, an echo in light.

Big Blue stilting thinks he has rendered himself invisible. He remains frozen in place the way rabbits freeze on the road, as if the car that will kill them is a snake whose simple reptile brain will be deceived by plain absence of motion. Heron believes—what? I am that rabbit-hungry snake? That I am Leonine? The Olympian Eagle whose talons are only folded out of sight? Or do I give myself more credit than I deserve and Heron only ignores me.

Even close approach will not dislodge him. He poses silent and uncaring, biblically unheedful ("*You shall have no gods before Me*"—and not giving a damn if you do). Finally, the one who must bow and back away is you. Such is his hegemony.

There is a lot to be said for the divinity of Great Blue Heron. Of all his kind, he alone braves the snow, the wind, the ice, and often pays the price. There comes a time when the deep of February arrives and the mercury turns crystalline, dull and misted in the glass, that most of the co-religionists of Heron pass.

Those that do survive range to deeper cover. I've never discovered exactly where they go. I know there are times when they live in the woods, hunting catlike for mice and voles when they can find them and for whatever else when they cannot. But among the flooded marshlands it is mostly fishes, and when that flood hardens over and fish cannot be found, cannot be had if they are found, what then does Heron do?

A flash a flare a wind of great wings, Heron's equally Significant Other flushes from the dry spartina leaping, a cool gray flame. Hardly the span of a tall man's arms between us, she settles like smoke and we stand eye to eye. Now it is me who must remain, riven by a flickering like fire.

The Mystery of Great Blue Heron and his mate is not solved by science or by faith. They appear, they vanish, they reappear. Therefore, if the feel of the marsh is emptiness and even the air is still, that is the time for patience. Do not hurry. Make no sound. Walking, use stealth. Watching, do not move. When Like pursues Like all things are revealed.

Good Neighbors Make Good Fences

An old Cyclone fence, posts and rails rusted and misshapen. You can see through it, hop over it. Probably knock it down bare-handed. Walk around it if you wanted but there is no need. The yard beyond grows rough and wild and no one left to tend or care. All this fence can tell you is, this little place used to belong, to someone long gone.

The new owner does not own. Unsympathetic to deed, meets, bounds, his nation is contained by range of flight alone. The fence is a convenience. The unkempt land below of value *because* it is unkempt. Talons grasped to